Quick, Fast, Done

Simple Time Management Secrets From
Some of History's Greatest Leaders

Bill Bodri

Top Shape Publishing, LLC
1135 Terminal Way Suite 209
Reno, NV 89502

ISBN-10: 0-9980764-0-6
ISBN-13: 978-0-9980764-0-9
Library of Congress Control Number: 2016917180

To arrange an author interview, please contact the author via wbodri@gmail.com.

DEDICATION

To My Mother. Without her constant love, compassion, guidance and teachings on how to get things done, none of these lessons would be possible for others. May she receive all the merit from this book.

TABLE OF CONTENTS

ACKNOWLEDGMENTS

I would like to thank Marshall Adair for his work in editing this book and for the effort he always puts into helping me with my literary efforts. Thanks also go to John Newtson for the endless hours we spent together trying to think up a title that might capture the message of the content.

1
Five Minutes Per Day

You often hear parents complaining about how busy they have become since their children were born. "There just doesn't seem to be enough time in the day to do anything anymore," is what many tell me. In response, I tell them about a method that my mother used in order take care of a busy household of six children and countless responsibilities. Using this very simple technique, she accomplished everything she had to do to run a busy household on a daily basis and still had time left over to relax at the end of the day.

The special "time management" or "productivity" trick that my mother religiously followed was to make and use *daily to-do lists*. Every night she would take a scrap of paper and make a list of all the things she had to do the very next day. She would adjust the list in the morning or during the day if something new came up that was sufficiently important.

All throughout the day my mother would then carry around this list of to-do items and whenever she finished one task she would run her pen through that item to cross it off.

Some people tick off items on a to-do list by marking the front of the line with a check mark or X, but that is the wrong way to do it. By crossing off items by running a line through them you actually make your list shorter as you complete items, and the increasingly shorter list over time produces a helpful positive psychological boost. As more and more items get finished your list gets shorter, and as it gets shorter you experience a psychological sense of completion that helps motivate you to finish off the list in total.

Crossing things off is the method that *The 4-Hour Workweek* author Tim Ferriss uses for his own to-do list. Every day he writes down five to six big task items on one note card, he crosses off each item as he completes it and then tears up the card when finished.

All day long my mom would work at finishing her task list, too, and if anything was left undone she would transfer the item over to the list for the next day. The basic idea is that one should always use lists to get things done.

The problem with my mother's method, however, was that it kept her busy at accomplishing tasks, but she wasn't progressing towards any larger objective such as accomplishing a specific goal or important target as you need to do in business. However, you can certainly create a system of to-do lists that help you be more proactive in this manner.

Let me show you how to create a proactive and extremely productive to-do list by telling you the story of one of the richest men in the twentieth century, Charles Schwab.

Charles Schwab used to work for Andrew Carnegie, who was also one of the richest men in the world during Schwab's day. In fact, Carnegie had initially hired Schwab as one of his managers and Schwab eventually ended up running the Carnegie Steel company, which later became U.S. Steel after it was bought out by J.P. Morgan. You can imagine all the management and labor issues that Schwab had to deal with on a daily basis all his life, and how busy Schwab must have been in running Carnegie Steel, then U.S. Steel and later Bethlehem Steel, the second largest steel producer in America at that time. This was a man who probably did not have much free time to himself.

If someone needed time management and productivity tools then that man was Charles Schwab.

One day Charles Schwab was meeting with his management consultant, Ivy Lee, who was asking for more business. Schwab told Lee, "We don't need more ideas, we need more execution of the ideas we already have. Show me a way to get more things done. If you can give me a way to get us to do the things we already know we have to do then I'll gladly pay you anything you ask."

Ivy Lee told him, "In 15 minutes I'll show you how you can get your organization doing at least 50% more. If all your executives use this method then you will have your wish. Use it, judge its value and then send me a check for whatever you think it's worth."

Here is the method Lee taught Schwab and his executives at Bethlehem Steel, which harkens back to my mother's very successful method of making daily to-do lists and then working to complete those tasks.

The Ivy Lee Method

First, at the end of each day you must write down the *five or six* most important things you need to do tomorrow. Not things that will make you busy that you have to do anyway, but the *important* things that will make you productive and move you ahead. Don't write down more than six tasks.

Next, prioritize these five or six items in order of their importance. We will talk about what is "important" in a moment.

Third, tomorrow morning when you arrive at work you

must concentrate on completing only the first task, which you have already decided is the most important. Work on completing that task until it is finished and only then move on to the second task.

Afterwards, approach every other item on your list in the same manner. First complete one task before you attempt to work on the next item of lesser importance.

At the end of the day, move any unfinished tasks to a new list of six items for tomorrow and then repeat this process every single day.

This approach was shared with the Bethlehem Steel management and the result was as follows. A short while later Lee received a check from Schwab for the unheard of amount of $25,000, which was the equivalent of $400,000 in today's dollars. The amount Schwab paid for this idea, after testing its effectiveness, was simply a king's ransom! In an accompanying note Schwab wrote to Lee that this simple productivity technique was the *most profitable lesson he had ever learned.*

The Keys to Success

This simple method will help you get things done quicker and is probably the simplest but most effective productivity system you will ever encounter. It requires just five minutes per day but discipline all day long, and it succeeds because it is simple and forces you to practice the power of *focus.*

The power of focus and concentration is the power of execution. It is the power of getting things done quickly. The individual who understands that he moves ahead because he attends to *important activities* rather than just busy activities, and who sticks to doing first those things that keep him moving him forward in productive output, is the person who will progress in life.

The keys to this technique's success are several. For instance, you should always prepare the list before the end of the day. If you prepare your list just before bedtime then while sleeping your mind will tend to start working to produce solutions for the tasks and challenges to be faced tomorrow. This is why important issues sometimes appear in your dreams.

The important directive, in any case, is to spend five minutes everyday making a short list of the most important items you need to accomplish tomorrow, which is certain to save you time the next day.

In compiling this list you must recognize that the "most important tasks" are the things that will have the biggest impact on your life and move you to the results you want. Unimportant tasks don't do that and so they don't have any priority. Urgent tasks don't necessarily fit that bill either. It is the important tasks which move you ahead!

Restricting yourself to a short list of six items also forces you to prioritize tasks in terms of their importance, and the brevity of just five or six items helps ensure that you can get things done. While a longer list of more items might keep you busy, it is unlikely to be completed or to represent the most productive use of your time, so when making this list you must focus on a short tally of just five or six items.

When you are making your to-do list and scheduling tasks the day before you should also estimate how long each item will take so that you can assign time slots to accomplishing each task in tomorrow's schedule. Planning for a task's execution means planning how much time you will dedicate to each to-do item and determining when its execution best fits into tomorrow's busy day. You also need to add up the time for all tasks to see if they fit into the next day's schedule. If not, the unimportant tasks can be delayed and particularly time consuming tasks can be broken up into smaller sub-tasks you perform across several days to make things doable.

Prioritizing the tasks means doesn't just mean

identifying the most important ones that will best move you toward your goals. It also means scheduling their completion so that the most important items are finished sooner rather than later. For instance, the extremely busy famous marketer Dan Kennedy sorts his Things-to-Do List by prioritizing tasks as A, B and C items, and he also prioritizes a People-to-Call list in order to make sure that he accomplishes the most important things first.

The general rule is always to do the most important things, most productive things or most difficult things first by scheduling them at the beginning of the day. By putting the most critical tasks at the beginning of the day you are ensuring that the most important things get done first. *Getting done first means that those things get done!*

Don't focus on doing easy tasks first, but remember the 80/20 rule that usually just 20% of tasks usually produce 80% of the results for getting you ahead. In other words, 20% of the effort produces 80% of the results you want. Hence, those 20% of items are usually the most productive or important tasks to focus on.

Human beings tend to procrastinate about doing difficult tasks or activities they don't like, which unfortunately are usually the most important ones for getting us ahead. As a result of putting them off, at the end of the day they still aren't completed (the delay usually continues forward in time as well) and then there isn't any time or energy left to finish off what's left to do. Therefore you must concentrate first and foremost on completing the activities with the most importance. To be productive and get things done, those things must assume the top priority every day.

You should also think of it this way. *If you do the most important thing first each day, then you will always get something important done!*

Difficult tasks always have to get done anyway so there is no real benefit from procrastinating and avoiding a difficult, unpleasant but important task. By staying focused on priority items first - no mater how you feel about them - you will always continue to be moving forward towards achieving your larger goals and objectives.

By doing those most important or difficult items at the beginning of the day, that is also when you usually have the most energy. Your energy and willpower tend to be highest at the beginning of the day, which means you will be able to provide your best efforts for your most important tasks if they are scheduled early. If your energy peaks at a different time of the day, then schedule your tasks accordingly by taking that into account.

It is at first frightening to begin the habit of doing the most important and sometimes most difficult (and thus distasteful) task first thing in the morning, but if you set up this routine then you will physically and emotionally get used to it and gradually become more productive over time. It is also a great habit to pass on to your children!

Benefits of the Method

What are the benefits of this short but simple productivity method?

First of all, *it actually works – largely because it is so simple!* Anyone can understand it so an entire organization can make use of it to increase its productivity, which is what happened at Bethlehem Steel. Sometimes people have to be forced into using this method so that it eventually becomes a natural habit, but it's a great skill to instill in others.

Second, by forcing yourself to make tough decisions on prioritizing activities you end up weeding out the non-essential tasks that would normally occupy your time without producing any significant results. Using this method therefore has the benefit of forcing you to work at getting results so that you get closer to your long-term or most important goals every day.

If you adhere to the 80/20 rule of focusing on the 20%

of activities that produce 80% of desired results then you will be relying on a method that keeps you steadily marching towards the results or consequences that are most important to your life. You'll stay focused on the things that matter.

This method requires you to stay concentrated and focused on completing one task at a time, and thus eliminates the problem of simultaneous multi-tasking that usually drops productivity to its knees. When you schedule tasks they become more likely to be completed, so it removes the indecision about what to do next and reduces procrastination or hesitation.

It also helps you *complete* tasks, for execution and completion is what it's all about. As Malcolm Forbes said, "One worthwhile task carried to a successful conclusion is worth half-a-hundred half-finished tasks."

Another benefit to this method is that scheduled activities make responsibilities seem more manageable and less overwhelming. That psychological also boost helps with the process of completion.

Furthermore, using this method will result in being able to leave work at the end of the day with less pressure or worries and you'll sleep better at night because you know that all your other activities will eventually get done in a timely manner. Using this method ensures that everything gets completed in time.

Most importantly, by creating a daily to-do list of prioritized items and then completing them in their order of importance (or as close to the order of importance as your schedule allows) you will be getting things done in a proactive manner and avoiding the need for last minute emergencies. Life and work will simply run smoother.

The Daily Business of Priorities

In his book, *The Pledge: Your Master Plan for an Abundant Life*, millionaire entrepreneur Michael Masterson explained how this simple practice of "doing first things first" by prioritizing tasks according to their importance changed his life. He wrote,

"It is the single best technique I know for change. And it's the fastest and easiest way to turn your life around if you are not happy with the way it's been going so far.

"Doing first things first. Is that what you do?

"Here's what I do:

- I get up early – never after 6:30 A.M.
- I get to work early – never later than 7:30 A.M.
- I spend my first hour doing a task that advances my most important goal.
- If I'm going strong, I spend the next hour doing the same thing. If not, I switch to a task that advances my second-most-important goal.
- I spend my third hour on another priority.
- Only after four hours of doing important work do I allow myself to deal with less important work and other people's urgencies.

"By the time most people start wandering into the office – between 8:30 and 9:00 – I've done at least an hour and sometimes two hours of work that is helping me achieve my important goals. Goals that correspond to my core values. Goals that will immensely improve my life.

"That's how I begin a very good day!

"I do this five days a week. And on weekends, I find at least two more hours each day to devote to my top priority. In a year, this averages to about 600 hours. Six hundred hours may not sound like much, but it is.

"Six hundred hours is fifteen 40-hour work weeks. That's almost four working months! Think about it."

Thus you now have a very simple method that is actually the most valuable time management and productivity method that I know. It is also the simplest method that I know. It helps you develop the habit of working on something until it is done, and strengthens your powers of focus and concentration.

The joy of completion you experience when you finish a single task or the entire list of items trains your mind to be successful.

Basically, this technique teaches persistence, grit, focus and concentration if you use it often enough.

I not only hope that you personally use it and share it with your colleagues, but that you also teach it to your children as my mother did to me along with my brothers and sisters. The greatest benefits of the method will accrue over time, so the largest bonanza will go to those who start using it early and consistently.

2
One Hour Per Week

Just one hour per week of study time, problem solving or review of your weekly actions and behavior can have a major impact on your life or business when you add up the hours. Just one hour per week!

The practice of spending just one hour per week to work on life issues or critical business issues will give you a chance to re-assess what and how you are doing whatever it is that you perceive as your mission.

An hour-long period of review provides you with the opportunity to introspect and see a larger picture, and by practicing that type of awareness on a regular basis you can learn how to step out of the daily stream of busy affairs and see a clearer picture of how to improve or perfect your life or business.

Earl Nightingale's Method of Self-Improvement

Where does the idea of "just one hour per week" come from? The idea was first introduced by motivational speaker Earl Nightingale a half-century ago as a means of self-improvement for busy people. It involves consistently studying a selected topic you want to master for an hour a day, every day, until you achieve basic mastery.

You can study something you are passionate about or something that might lead to a better job or second source of income. You might choose to work on developing some special talent or skill. For business you might choose to study the industry you are in or the job you perform so that you become indispensable at work and move up the corporate ladder.

Just a month or two of extra daily study can set you apart from your colleagues at work because it will enable you to develop knowledge or skills others don't have that might earn you a raise or promotion. This is one way to change your life in a positive fashion, especially if you are also making to-do lists and performing regular goal setting activities. Think of how combining these things together will empower you to excel.

In just six months of concentrated daily study, at just one hour per day, you can usually understand the basics of almost any topic and begin to really master it. It is said that knowledge is power and value compounds over time, so if you spend an hour a day mastering some new skill or knowledge then in time you might be able to rejuvenate your career, create a new job or source of income, or just achieve greater overall life satisfaction.

Life Review on a Weekly Basis

In his book *How to Win Friends and Influence People*, Dale Carnegie told the story of one of the most important financiers in America, the president of an important Wall Street bank, who admitted that he owed most of his career success to a particular style of one hour per week sessions. The banker, addressing one of Carnegies' classes on self-improvement, described the method:

"For years I have kept an engagement book showing

all the appointments I had during the day. My family never made any plans for me on Saturday night, for the family knew I devoted a part of each Saturday evening to the illuminating process of self-examination and review and appraisal. After dinner I went off by myself, opened my engagement book, and thought over all the interviews, discussions and meetings that had taken place during the week. I asked myself:

"'What mistakes did I make that time?'

"'What did I do that was right – and in what way could I have improved my performance?'

"'What lessons can I learn from that experience?'

"I often found that this weekly review made me very unhappy. I was frequently astonished at my own blunders. Of course, as the years passed, these blunders became less frequent. Sometimes I was inclined to pat myself on the back a little after one of these sessions. This system of self-analysis, self-education, continued year after year, did more for me than any other one thing I ever attempted.

"It helped me improve my ability to make decisions—and it aided me enormously in all my contacts with people. I cannot recommend it too highly."

This banker wasn't the only one who discovered that taking one hour per week to review his previous week's efforts was a great way to help him eliminate his errors, stay in line with his core values and accomplish his life goals. In his book *Make it Big! 49 Rules for Building a Life of Extreme Success,* the real estate developer Frank McKinney explained how he would take time off every week to review his life and his business:

"Every Saturday afternoon … I sit down with the previous week's chart and a copy of my personal vision statement. I review my vision statement first, to remember the big picture of what I want my life to be about this year. Then I look at the previous week's accomplishments and what hasn't gotten done, and I ask, 'How was this week?

How did I approach things? What did I do well? What did I do wrong? Where did I fail, not only professionally but personally? Where did I not live up to my personal vision statement?' Then I ask the most important questions: 'What can I learn from this? How can I be a better person next time?' I write the answers to all those questions on the back of the previous week's chart. Once I have done my introspection, then—and only then—am I ready to plan a new week. Weekly introspection gives me the ability to grasp everything that's going on around me and, for the most part, to feel in control of the direction of my life."

The One-hour Productivity Meeting

The power of just one hour per week, when used in the right way, can propel your life forward. The basic idea, as humble as "one hour" sounds, can be used to dramatically affect business profits as well.

For instance, many years ago the marketing genius behind Intel, Apple Computer and Genentech was asked what was the key to effective marketing, and he responded, "one hour per week." He explained that to get more effective marketing he would pull a handful of people into a meeting room for one hour every week and discuss what they could do to make the company's marketing efforts more impactful.

As with the daily to-do lists where you concentrate on accomplishing the most important tasks first, he focused on asking for ideas about *just the important things* that might propel the company's marketing efforts to better results.

Every week you can call a similar such meeting for any department of your company. You might pose questions like, "What do we need to do in order to cut shipping costs," and try to direct peoples' mental efforts to finding solutions to pressing problems. One-hour meetings of this nature are not meant to keep you busy but are designed for brevity to push you ahead.

If you restrict the amount of time you spend on an activity but still require the positive end result, you tend to cut out useless chatter and become more productive, so there is no reason to drag out these meetings. Time constraints usually tend to sharpen the mind and increase your output.

In fact, the industrialist Henry Ford, founder of the Ford Motor Company, discovered the principle that when he decreased the daily working time at his plants from ten to eight hours and shortened the work week from six to five days then plant productivity increased. Often you become far more productive if you reduce overtime (or excessive chatter) and allow yourself just a finite amount of time to complete tasks.

The idea of using a certain amount of time each week to increase productivity and thereby move ahead is even found in Frank Bettger's famous book, *How I Raised Myself from Failure to Success in Selling*.

Bettger wrote, "If you are having trouble getting yourself organized, if you want to increase your ability to think, and do things in the order of their importance, remember there is only one way: Take more time to think and do things in order of their importance. Set aside one day as self-organization day, or a definite period each week. The whole secret to freedom from anxiety over not having enough time lies not in working more hours, but in proper planning of those hours."

Just one hour per week on a personal or business basis is short enough that the time can be spared, and can certainly be used to review past actions, plan the week ahead or solve problems, roadblocks and challenges that prevent you from progressing further.

If you want more productivity in your life, set aside a time for concentrated work, a time for planning, and a time for reviewing what you are doing.

The One-Hour Process Improvement Meeting

One of the most profitable ways to increase productivity in one hour is by employing a special type of weekly workshop designed to help solve all sorts of challenging problems in an organization.

How should you run such a meeting? Let me give you the brilliant technique of Chet Homes, author of *The Ultimate Sales Machine*. The methodology is as follows.

First, call all the relevant people into a room and appoint someone to lead the group, which is usually the chief manager or head honcho. Write down the particular problem to be solved (topic to be discussed) on a whiteboard, such as "What do we have to do to improve sales?" or "How can we raise the product's quality?" or "How can we get more visitors?"

Next comes the creative brainstorming part of the session, and if you are particularly interested in brainstorming and creativity methods then I suggest you seek out the Canadian CBC News feature of Doug Hall and his Eureka Ranch, which is superb for the many methods it demonstrates.

For the solution-seeking (brainstorming) part of the meeting, ask everyone to write down on their pad of paper as many ideas as possible that might solve the issue being discussed. Stress that everyone must think of *at least three ideas minimum*.

No one is allowed to call out their ideas, but must quietly write them down on paper. Even the leader of the session must write down his three (or more) ideas.

Give the group no more than three minutes to do this.

After the three minutes are up (sometimes two minutes are all that is required), the leader will ask each person in turn to tell their ideas. As they spoken, the leader will write each idea on the chalkboard in a summarized format.

During this part of the meeting, discussion is limited. The point is to create a list of possible solution ideas as quickly as possible without much discussion. When ideas are being offered, all negativity and criticisms from group members are also forbidden because they would stifle the group's creative flow, and so the offered ideas are simply recorded on the whiteboard without much discussion. When voting on the best ideas the bad ones will naturally be eliminated from consideration without embarrassing people or hurting anyone's feelings.

Basically you simply record all the ideas on the board in shorthand form as quickly as possible and then the next step is to arrive at a group consensus of the best ones to try in order of importance, doability, or whatever other criteria is most relevant to the issue.

The criteria as to what are the "best" ideas would certainly differ according to the situation. "Best" might be defined as the ideas most likely to work, easiest to implement, or likely to have the biggest impact, quickest impact, most permanent impact, least cost, least disruptiveness, highest visibility and so on.

The way to arrive at a group consensus of the best ideas, which is the next step, is as follows.

Since all the ideas are written on the board for everyone to see, ask each person to pick their top three choices from this long list. Give the group just 30 seconds for everyone to rate the ideas and then ask in turn that each pick their top three choices in order of importance (preference for biggest impact, most likely to work, etcetera).

Now you will poll the group for their considerations. The leader will go around to each person in turn and ask them about their choices. No one can escape! Everyone will be asked their opinion.

On the board the leader will mark slashes next to each idea to indicate how much a person likes it. Make three slashes for someone's top choice, two slashes for their second choice and one slash for their third choice. This means that each idea on the board will start collecting a row of slashes which indicates its popularity.

After everyone's priorities have been given, add up the

number of slashes next to each idea. The total number of slashes for each idea will represent the group's conclusion as to the most important (most feasible, profitable, impactful etc.) things to do. The highest number of marks will represent the collective judgment for the best idea, the second highest total identifies the second best idea, and so on.

Tally up the numbers for everything, but as with the daily to-do list that focuses only on the top five to six items to act upon you will also find that you should stay focused and concentrate on executing only the top tier of best ideas.

Having done all of this polling, everyone will feel happier because important issues are being addressed, everyone gets their voice heard, and people feel more important for having contributed. The meeting forces a large sharing of ideas, and big breakthroughs come from sharing. You can never predict who will give the best ideas, and solutions to pressing problems often come from the most unexpected individuals!

Since the meeting also openly arrives at a group consensus that everyone sees, studies show that this will help with everyone's commitment to trying the various approaches suggested, especially when they are untested.

Furthermore, since this method focuses on identifying the 20% of activities that will likely produce 80% of results then it also becomes a means that might strongly enhance a company's profits and productivity. This is a method for improving your bottom line!

Now you basically have an idea of what needs to be done. The next thing is to determine how to do it, namely how to implement the action steps you want to try.

It is very important to keep a record of these idea generation workshops because not all the ideas will work, but later other people will want to see what you ended up thinking and trying. If you keep the record of meeting notes in a readily available binder then other people, and in particular an organization's leaders, can always look back to see what was discussed and use that record to update themselves and keep tabs on progress.

Chet Holmes said that he was able to run simultaneously several different magazines for Charlie Munger, Warren Buffett's billionaire investment partner, and could keep track of countless management and improvement efforts going on in each of these entities just by reviewing such binders.

Any new employee or member of a group can also quickly read through the records of these meetings and update themselves on what has been thought and tried, which will help them get up to speed quickly. This will cut training costs tremendously by transmitting the best practices and knowledge base of any organization extremely fast.

These one hour per week meetings are a way of proactively solving problems rather than just reacting to them. They are a means of taking an organization forward.

As Michael Gerber, author of *The E-Myth* stresses, you should be working *on* your business rather than *in* your business because that is the key to growing it. Therefore instituting a process of weekly one-hour meetings that focus on determining solutions rather than just discussing problems can help you do just that.

The Implementation Process

Once you have selected the best ideas from your workshop group, the issue that now arises is how to implement them. This is where the five W's must be determined – What? Who? When? Where? Why?

Don't forget How? and How Much? as well.

The point is that the accountability of trial execution must now be assigned to relevant parties and the expectations of success aroused.

The mnemonic SMART is often applied to this process because it summarizes all the aspects quite nicely. You want Specific and Measurable action steps to be taken. You want the group to Agree upon these achievable, attainable goals, which happens naturally because of the polling process by which they were derived. You want to decide who will be Responsible for creating the Receivables or Results, and you want to set relevant Time deadlines or schedules for actions if necessary.

How will your team implement the top ideas you just arrived at? If necessary, once again ask your team how they are going to implement the idea during a workshop mode. Have everyone write down their idea as to the perfect or ideal structure for implementing each of the top ideas.

After being given some time, the leader should again poll individuals one at a time for their ideas and write them on the whiteboard. In this case, however, the leader should start out by first polling someone known to have good solution or solid implementation skills so that everything that follows will from the outset assume a higher standard.

As they are writing down the ideas the leader should work through them, guiding the group and shaping them as things go until he establishes the optimal structure using everyone's ideas. He has to develop a conceptual solution procedure of "here is what we will try" for each of the top ideas (if that is required).

As stated, accountability must be assigned. At this stage the group (or leader) must determine who will be responsible for what activities as well as how, when, where and so forth. Names must be named as well as responsibilities defined and deadlines established.

These things should all be documented and sent out in a memo so that it is easy to audit how the implementation efforts are going. As a manager yourself, if you don't follow up and ask how things went, if you don't monitor the results of this process and continue to try to improve on the execution of an initial idea then the whole procedure becomes useless. People only respect what you inspect so you have to keep tabs on group efforts at implementation.

In next week's meeting the leader can collect feedback about all the various implementation efforts and how things went. This is a time to ask each person precisely what they did that worked or didn't work so that the feedback can be used to improve the process. With the new input you can then rework any procedures as necessary.

Some ideas don't work the first time you try them, but that doesn't mean they should immediately be abandoned. A leader who keeps pushing for incremental improvements can eventually turn an idea that is an initial failure into something quite profitable if they have the right sort of wisdom.

The point here is not just to get the best ideas from a group for some type of improvement, but to continue revisiting the topic again and again and coming up with new things you might try until the goal of building continuous incremental improvement occurs.

A leader can certainly shape and guide the ideas coming out of a strategy session to the ones he prefers, but please remember that one useful aspect to the process is that subordinates tend to have a higher commitment to objectives they set for themselves than to those imposed on them by another person. The process of jointly working together to discover things you should try has this and other unspoken benefits.

This whole process has similarities to Peter Drucker's teachings on "management by objectives" where specific goals or objectives are defined by a leader and then an organization's members figure out how to achieve these objectives.

A smart company might require that every department use this method to solve pressing problems and make the results publicly available in a binder so that others can at a glance see what has been discussed, attempted and is working versus what was tried and failed.

As already noted, people respect what you inspect so there is a great benefit to public tracking as a means for showing everyone how the group is progressing at bringing everything forward.

This particular strategy of "just one hour per week" can be used for business or personal life. An athlete or musician might also use a weekly hour-long meeting with a coach to focus solely on becoming better at one particular part of his/her routine. You might spend one hour per week doing visualization practice in order to master some skill. If you are a family, a weekly one-hour meeting between spouses might focus on how to cut costs or improve family finances.

Typically in business a dedicated one hour per week session focuses exclusively on just one topic of interest. With fifty-two weeks available in a year, you should try to use these techniques in a regular system for improving your business or life one topic at a time and thus help move things forward. Most people would love a systematic method for personal self-improvement or for discovering business process improvements and this is one such method.

As with any new thing you try, there initially may be failures in using the technique, but don't give up. Try again and again and always analyze and improve on your failures.

3
Monthly Regularity

Spending one hour per week to review your personal behavior over the last seven days or to proactively work on specific business issues can be the one major thing that regularly improves your life or moves your business ahead.

One hour per week can become your most solid means for self-improvement or process improvement depending on how you use that one hour.

On a personal basis you might use regular weekly one-hour sessions to plan the week ahead just as you might analyze the week in review in order to identify past mistakes and prevent them from reoccurring in the future. Such one-hour sessions can easily be made into a regular schedule and if used properly will help you continually move towards your long-term goals and dreams in life.

Businesses usually need more meetings than just one per week, and many business meetings will normally last far more than one hour. The common sense rule is not to be bound by rigidity but to be flexible in your ways and use whatever you must in order to run your business. That being said, there is a great benefit to regular monthly routines that can augment your daily and weekly efforts.

People have often asked me whether there is a best, optimal or natural frequency for scheduling various types of meetings because they don't want too many and they also don't want too few. They just want their organizations to run well without much friction, and they don't want to get bogged down in too many meetings.

The Natural Meeting Schedule

The best proposal I have ever found for an optimal meeting schedule is to follow the natural rhythm of the year just as you do in regular life. This means scheduling meetings on a regular weekly, monthly, quarterly and yearly basis. Thus there would be daily, weekly, quarterly and annual meetings that you might hold for an organization.

Let's go over the typical nature of these meetings based on a natural scheduling frequency, as suggested in the excellent book, *Mastering the Rockefeller Habits*.

Annually you can hold an important two to three day retreat, or much simpler meeting, where the chief executive and executive group (or the entire company) jointly determines the larger goals for the year. An alternative other than setting particular goals is to set a particular *theme* for a year. However, in the *Rockefeller Habits* plan, you try to pick five main priorities for the year, and focus on a major priority each quarter.

For instance, Facebook founder Mark Zuckerberg on a personal level holds himself to a "personal challenge" every year, and this concept can be applied to business as a theme or challenge for the year. One year Zuckerberg set himself the goal of wearing a tie every day. Another year he set himself the goal of learning Chinese. Yet another year he set himself the goal of learning to be thankful for the food he eats.

A yearly "theme" for a business might revolve around quality control or improving customer service. There are many issues that might be chosen as a yearly theme because of their relevance to a business.

Just as a year contains four natural seasons (winter, spring, summer and autumn) that exhibit very different temperaments, the four quarters of the annual business cycle can exhibit very different profit, cost and customer behavioral patterns. Since the nature of company activities might have to vary in quality, pace and tempo in response, quarterly meetings (which match the natural segments of the earth's seasons) might be used as natural review points to chop up any yearly targets into smaller pieces. An accounting year also focuses on quarterly reporting periods so the four quarters are a perfect time for reviewing the progress of various business endeavors over the past three months and can be used for initiating new quarterly priorities and challenges for the next 120-day period.

Monthly meetings are perfect for matching the typical accounting timetable used for closing the books, preparing financial statements and issuing paychecks. Thus they are a natural time to review what's working and what isn't (in business or life) on a more short-term basis.

Weekly meetings at most firms often involve some type of problem solving, reporting, analysis and scheduling functions as well as tactical decisions for implementing various plans. When used as one hour per week workshops on a continuous basis you can pick a new topic for consideration each week and slowly, through its decisions, achieve huge improvements in outcomes over the course of a year.

If you have ever watched the TV series *L.A. Law* then you know that every episode starts with the law firm's daily morning meeting, which lasts just a few minutes. The lawyers and partners meet in an executive conference room and in just a few minutes find out what is going on with everyone's case load. Each lawyer reports on the status of their cases and there is also a brief notification of any important problems or issues at the firm in general.

Longer discussions are arranged at this meeting but tabled for private sessions between just the relevant parties so that the dialogue doesn't waste everybody else's time.

Daily update meetings at a typical firm usually last no more than 5-15 minutes. They are typically quick because they usually just give a reading on the pulse of the business and are used to rapidly clear issues that might clog the weekly meetings. As a result, in some firms the meetings are run with the participants standing up behind their chairs just to remind everyone not to linger or waste time on extra dialogue.

To have everyone stand for a short meeting in order to emphasize brevity is a powerful technique. Did you know that Winston Churchill, Charles Dickens, and Ernest Hemingway all did their writing while standing up in order to become more productive?

Short daily meetings are often used to pass out daily business measurements and indicators. People update others on the status or specifics about other meetings, activities, tasks, accomplishments, or news from customers or markets. They are often a place where people can raise their hand for assistance on certain issues but where the nitty-gritty details are worked out in discussions elsewhere.

Every company will naturally have a different meeting schedule, and the content of those meetings will vary considerably from firm to firm, which goes without saying. The big question, though, is how you link them all together into a cohesive whole to help improve the firm and push it forwards. Also, how can you use this frequency of annual, quarterly, monthly, weekly and daily reviews for your life?

Frank McKinney's Top-Down Approach

Perhaps the best example of a comprehensive system of special meetings you might hold during a year comes from real estate developer Frank McKinney's book, *Make it Big! 49 Rules for Building a Life of Extreme Success.* McKinney felt that the entire tone of the year for his business had to come from a vision statement he annually forged for the year ahead. With that yearly vision, he had to formulate a set of periodic reviews that would help him accomplish his personal and business goals and stay on track toward manifesting his larger goals as well.

As I explained in *How to Create a Million Dollar Unique Selling Proposition* about product, service and business design, entrepreneurs should always set a unique vision for their business. They have to work out its essential purpose and the messaging they wish to broadcast to all customers, clients, employees and suppliers. McKinney also feels that a vision is what sets entrepreneurs apart from the workers who just do their job for a paycheck and then go home at the end of the day. A vision can give true meaning to work and make it into a larger purpose or calling that improves the lives of others – and makes the world a better place.

This harkens back to the famous vision story of a man who came upon a construction site where three masons were working. The man asked the first mason, who seemed unhappy at his work, "What are you doing?" and received the response, "I am laying bricks." He asked the same question of the second mason, who seemed more interested in what he was doing, and was told, "I am building a wall." When he finally asked the third mason, who was humming as he worked on a wall that looked a little bit straighter than the rest, the mason replied, "I am building a cathedral."

Three different men were all doing the same job, but because of different personal attitudes as to their ultimate purpose their lives were emotionally richer or poorer and their work output was quite different.

Just as "character is destiny," how and what you think about the purpose of your business and life will ultimately have great power in transforming their outcomes. Setting yourself the bar of a higher purpose in anything you do will have a positive effect on your attitude and cause you to want to excel. On the other hand, a lower purpose or none at all will have a negative effect on your motivation and thus dampen the outcomes you are after.

In order to provide his business with a higher mission other than that of just making money, once a year McKinney would set aside some time to review the purpose of his business and life and try to see them from a higher perspective. Every year he would go through the exercise of hammering out a core ideology of purpose and values that embodied a higher service mission other than just profits, and then sought some way to align his goals, strategy, tactics and actions around that higher mission. The method he used of maintaining alignment throughout the year shows how to link all our various schedules together.

He wrote, "This simple planning process—setting aside one weekend a year to create a new personal vision statement, and then taking a couple of hours each Saturday to establish the goals that will help me turn that vision into reality—has been the bedrock underlying my success for the past 10 years. Once I started doing this, I found a marked change in my life and in my results. Sure, I was accomplishing more, since I was taking the time to plan my week. But more than that, I was linking my weekly goals to the vision of who I wanted to be. ...

"A personal vision and mission statement is the agreement you make with yourself that this is who you want to be, how you want to act, what you will and won't do, and how you want to appear in the world. It's also a living, breathing document that will change over the years. I know there are some people who like to create 5- and 10-year plans for their lives, but I'm not one of them. Sure, I can have a sense of who I want to be 10 years from now, but I have found that redoing my vision every year keeps it fresh. It allows me to take into account the progress I have or haven't made and set my direction based on what I see as my next step. After all, I have the big picture of my highest calling ... that pulls me toward my ultimate future much more strongly than a 5- or 10-year plan. ...

"Having a mission or vision statement for your business is the first step. Tying it to your goals is the next. Do your quarterly or yearly goals have anything to do with your mission? ...

"The last step is to make sure your daily efforts represent the goals you've set and the vision you've created. When your business spends its days pursuing goals based on your corporate vision, your customers as well as the business community will see you as having integrity. And isn't that the kind of reputation you want?"

Frank McKinney's testimony reveals a perfect way to weld all these different schedules and review periods together. It is a challenge to keep to a higher purpose in life and stay on track when you are in the trenches just as it is a challenge to remain profitable and grow a business when surrounded by lots of competition. However, just as oxygen is important for life but not the point of life, profitability is necessary for business but should not be considered the premier purpose of the business.

Profit is necessary for a firm's survival, and people certainly start businesses in order to make a profit, but if you want to raise yourself to a higher purpose then profit should really be viewed as the means whereby the business can continue to provide a *service mission* to others, which is its higher calling. As the story of the three masons showed, the purpose of a business is to provide a service mission, and profit is a necessity for the business to be able to serve that function.

Using this story as a guide, one of the important things we can do in life rather than just work at our career is step back on a weekly, quarterly and even yearly basis and ask ourselves, "Is my life on track? Are my goals worthy of me? Are my efforts having meaning? Is what I'm doing part of a higher mission?"

If you determine that your life has gone off course you

should then start working toward creating a new life and fortune.

How do you tell if you are on track? Just ask yourself some of these questions.

What do I want my life to be about? Where are my actions taking me? What is the purpose of my career or business? Do I have energy when I get up in the morning and go about my daily business? Do I feel good about what I am doing for a living? Are the activities I'm engaged in worthy of my life force and talents? Is the road I'm on propelling me toward an inspiring future? Is this road adding to my life force or robbing me of energy? Am I living with integrity?

These questions will help you decide if your life is on track or if you need to start making some significant fundamental changes.

The Importance of Regularity

What you should note about the periodicity of McKinney's methodology is the regularity of the process. He shows you how to set up a regular yearly routine of interlocking reviews that match with the natural cycles of weeks, months, and quarters of a year. The regularity of his entire process and its great benefits reminds me strongly of the unspoken benefits of family traditions, which are also usually held on a regular basis.

Family traditions, as you know, are ritualistic actions and behaviors that your family engages in again and again. Most families have their own periodic traditions such as the yearly Thanksgiving dinner, Christmas season get-together, regular Sunday meal, weekly family television night, newlywed date night of the week and other regular celebrations.

Family gatherings held on a regular basis do not just create wonderful lasting memories for everyone. They add to the rhythm and seasonality of life, add meaning to the passage of time, offer us comfort and security and help solidify family culture. Basically, the regularity of family traditions is important in building successful families.

Bill Bonner's *Family Fortunes: How to Build Family Wealth and Hold on to It for 100 Years* reveals yet another annual tradition that you might care to emulate for your family's benefit, which is an annual Family Meeting. This is a time when everyone gets together and shares what they are doing, and where the family as a whole works through certain issues such as solidifying what it feels is its own mission in the world. This is where a family can also coordinate its philanthropic impulses and discuss issues that affect the fate of the generations.

Confucius said that to help the world you must first start by working on yourself. Saving the world starts with saving yourself first, meaning you must decide to set out upon the road of self-perfection. In Asia this is called self-cultivation, and Confucius called it cultivating your own person. This is what Frank McKinney's efforts represent when viewed through the lens of self-cultivation, self-regulation, self-improvement, self-actualization or self-perfection. You start helping or "saving" others only when you first begin working on yourself.

Confucius said that only after cultivating yourself can you then have a positive impact on your family, which will be affected by your efforts. If all families in turn adopt this sort of behavior and a common aspiration to cultivate higher values and ethics, a state will then seem to become better governed as a natural effortless result. If all states in the world become filled with such families then Confucius claimed that the entire world would find peace.

Frank McKinney's appraisal method for self-improvement and business advancement offers lessons in how to link together various types of efforts for the larger goal of prosperity in life. For families, the constancy of family traditions can be used in the same way rather than just for the purpose of binding its members together. The regularity of family bonding through regular traditions throughout the year connects us with our past, imparts values and cohesion to family members, and therefore helps families shape a sense of identity. With that joint identity as a family we can aspire towards higher ideals for society.

Just as the periodic regularity of family traditions helps families stay strong and make progress in ethics and affluence, the periodic review processes we've gone over (which can take other shapes and forms) can also be used to shape your character, life and fortune in a positive way.

4
HELPFUL PRACTICES AND PROCESSES

There is a legendary study on goal setting bandied about that involves the graduating class of either Harvard University or Yale University depending on who writes about it. You can find the legend in Mark McCormick's *What They Don't Teach You at Harvard Law School.* The basic story is that the Ivy graduates of an upper class academic program were asked whether they had clear written goals and plans for their future rather than just keeping everything in their heads or having no plans whatsoever.

The very popular conclusion of this mythical study was that people who set clear, written goals for their future and make concrete plans to accomplish them ultimately end up with more income than those who don't. Because they crystallize their goals into written plans they tend to actually get what they want out of life so it's not surprising to find that they wind up having more money, free time and fun than those who have no specific goals or simply don't put them down in writing. The go-getters get the glory.

In other words, those who crystallize their goals, (whether for life or business) into written plans and targets and then work to achieve them *tend to have a higher probability of achieving them.* The net result usually *is* more money, more free time, more fun in life and more accomplishment!

Although this conclusion came from a mythical Harvard or Yale University study that cannot be found, most motivational experts actually believe in these conclusions. So do I.

According to a well-known study done by Gail Matthews at Dominican University, those people who wrote down their goals accomplished significantly more than those who did not write down their goals. Specifically, those people who wrote down their goals, shared this information with a friend and then sent updates to that friend were 33% more successful in accomplishing those targets than individuals who merely formulated goals.

For this study, Matthews had collected a list of 149 participants from six different countries which included a variety of entrepreneurs, lawyers, managers, educators, marketers, bankers, human service providers, healthcare artists, and other professionals.

The participants were assigned into five different groups as follows. Group 1 participants were asked to think about their goals, Group 2 members were asked to write about their goals, Group 3 members wrote about their goals and formulated action commitments, Group 4 went a step further by formulating action commitments *and* sent their goals and action commitments to a supportive friend, and Group 5 did everything Group 4 had to do but took the extra step of sending out a weekly progress report to their supportive friend as well.

The conclusions of the study were as follows.

Those in Group 5 who sent weekly progress reports to their friends accomplished significantly more than everyone else, which speaks to the power of accountability. Those who made a public commitment of their goals to their friends also accomplished significantly more than those who simply wrote action commitments or didn't write down their goals. Lastly, those who wrote down their goals accomplished significantly more than those who did not.

Persuasion expert Kevin Hogan also reported on a marketing study that also tends to confirm the monetary benefits of setting goals. A survey of independent sales people revealed that those who do not set sales goals at all earn the least among all sales people, while those who set general earnings goals earn twice as much as those setting no goals, and those setting specific goals earn three times as much as those who set no goals at all.

In *Thinking, Fast and Slow* Nobel Prize winner Daniel Kahneman reported that goals do make a difference. In a study of 12,000 seventeen or eighteen year olds who rated their financial goals on a scale of one to four, twenty years later each point on the scale was found to represent $12,000 to $14,000 of extra income. Furthermore, it was found that those who had wanted income and got it were significantly more satisfied with their lives.

Researchers Edwin Locke and Gary Latham also analyzed the performance of over 40,000 goal setters and found that setting goals consistently leads to better performance than just urging people to do their best. Once again, a study has therefore showed that setting goals can help you achieve better outcomes.

Research in general has shown that the poorest performers of activities don't set goals at all but just do the work asked of them. Better performers set general goals and try to achieve generally good outcomes.

The "best performers" in many areas, however, don't seem to set goals about outcomes but about the *process* of achievement. They focus on doing their absolute best in a process that produces an outcome. In order to improve their final results they therefore focus on how they can get better and improve their skills or performance on some specific element of their work; they focus on getting better at the process in order to excel.

Write It Down

These findings all harken back to our earliest rule that for the best success at achieving your goals and tasks you must always write them down and create some type of feedback, monitoring, measuring, evaluation or accounting (accountability) system to help keep you on track towards their accomplishment. You will also need willpower - a continual force of motivation or commitment - so that there is always an inspiration for you to keep working on those goals.

If something remains in your mind and never makes it onto paper then it is simply a mental wish, but once written down it becomes an actual plan. Writing an idea down causes it to leave the realm of thoughts and enter the material plane. However, at this point an idea by itself still won't change your life until you work at it through the path of perspiration.

While activity is what matters in the end, the studies show that *writing down one's goals* definitely enhances the process of goal achievement. It basically helps things get done! This is why I always advise everyone to create a yearly journal or calendar of annual goals so that you start working on actual manifestation plans and have a means of actually working towards them. You have to write these things down!

Writing something down makes it part of the reality of the external world rather than something that remains in the realm of thoughts. The benefit of writing things down is that your thoughts and plans become better crystalized, lessons learned are remembered and put to use (because they are incorporated into what you write down), and positive strategies of achievement start to develop.

For a better life you should take whatever vision you have and turn it into a written description of concrete goals you need to work on. Then you should set up a scheduled process for achievement and a written monitoring system that measures how well you are progressing towards the final attainment.

The pain of not achieving a goal is often just as important a motivating influence as the pleasure you expect to feel on accomplishing it, therefore a monitoring (accounting) system that records failures as well as successes will help you to produce more achievements in the long run.

Visualize It

The idea behind the whole process of setting goals and working towards their achievement is that a dominating idea, plan, purpose or aspiration can be held in the mind as an inspirational or motivational objective until it is finally achieved.

One little-known trick to help with the achievement effort concerns the power of visualization. If you repeatedly visualize in your mind that you achieve a goal then the constant rehearsal (via the visualized imagery of success) will help move you forward to its achievement.

For instance, studies in sports training have shown that if you visualize yourself attaining a skill then the effort will help you attain it. In sports training athletes are commonly taught to build a vivid, high definition mental blueprint of a desired outcome through visualization practice, and repeated visualizations of those perfected skills and outcomes actually helps the athletes attain those skills.

Similarly, if you visualize that you succeed at an ordinary goal in life it will help you create new neurological pathways (neural circuits) in your brain that are associated with its achievement.

One example of this is that Arnold Schwarzenegger won the Mr. Olympia bodybuilding contest four times and the Mr. Universe contest five times. He employed various training regimens and training exercises (such as ballet) to do so. Most people don't know that he also practiced visualizing that his muscles and body were in ideal shape while exercising. In other words, he used visualization practice to help shape his muscles and he felt this helped him win these championships.

Schwarzenegger also explained, "I visualized myself being and having what it was I wanted. Before I won my first Mr. Universe title, I walked around the tournament like I owned it. I had won it so many times in my mind that there was no doubt I would win it. Then I moved on to the movies, the same thing. I visualized myself being a famous actor and earning big money. I just knew it would happen."

There are many sports studies which demonstrate the power of visualization in helping people master skills and achieve winning outcomes, so it has become an accepted practice in elite sports training for a long time. For instance, sports competitors are commonly taught how to vividly imagine running the entire course of a race as a type of practice rehearsal, such as skiers who are taught to imagine seeing the skiing of a difficult racing course as if seen through their own eyes. This is called *internal imagery* whereas seeing yourself complete a race, as if you were watching a video of yourself performing the activity, is called *external imagery*.

There are benefits to both types of visual imagination. Visualizing that your bones begin healing faster after they are broken, wherein you also feel the body's energy around the bone injury, is another type of internal visualization practice that actually helps by combining images and sensations together. If you recite sounds throughout the area as if coming from within it, such as "Hreem," this helps, too.

Studies have definitely shown the effectiveness of visualization at improving sports performance. For instance, at the Olympic Training Center in Colorado thirty-two golfers practiced their putting skills every day for one week. A first group visualized all their physical motions and the ball going into the hole because of their putt. A second group visualized the ball veering away from the cup while a third group performed regular putting practice without any visualization efforts. The final results were that Group 2's putting accuracy went down by 21%, Group 3's putting skills went up by 11% while Group 1's skills increased by 30%.

In 1991, a study of 121 field hockey players found that players who just did physical practice improved their shooting skills by 70% while those who used visualized imagery improved their goal shooting by 160%.

Similarly in a basketball study, one team practiced shooting basketballs for four hours per day. Another team practiced shooting for three hours and visualized making perfect shots for just one hour. The second team scored 26% more than the first due to the addition of its visualization practice.

Such is the power of visualization for helping you improve your skills and outcomes. You should expect that its power can be used in other areas of life as well.

Rehearsing a skill over and over again in your mind using inner visualization helps create neurological patterns in your brain that will help you learn and master the movements you are visualizing. That is why golfers use videos to repeatedly review the "perfect" swings of golfers they wish to emulate.

Now just as your subconscious mind works on finding solutions to problems when you go to sleep at night, and just as visualizing the perfect performance of a sports activity helps you master the skills of execution, when you visualize yourself completing a desired goal (outcome) on a regular basis then a complete visual picture of that effort (with all five senses) that is regularly refreshed will give your subconscious mind something to work on in terms of figuring out how to achieve it.

You absolutely cannot achieve goals just by visualizing

the end result nor magically attract an outcome to you through the power of visualization. However, there is a great benefit to visualizing yourself completing all the steps that it will take to do something.

The Napoleon Hill Method

Many of the ideas for using visualization and mental imagery to achieve your goals were first put forth in Napoleon Hill's book, *Think and Grow Rich*. This book is so popular that it has sold over 70 million copies worldwide and has been read by more millionaires than almost any other book in existence.

In addition to popularizing countless success tools (such as visualization practice, mastermind groups, affirmations, adhering to sexual discipline to conserve energy, channeling the power of the subconscious mind, etc.) to help people achieve success in life, it provides an overall philosophy of achievement with the how-to steps of attainment. Napoleon Hill derived these lessons by interviewing countless great leaders - the wealthiest and most successful men of his time - introduced to him by Andrew Carnegie.

Hill explained that the very first step of successful endeavor is to fix your mind on exactly what it is you desire. Create a goal picture in your mind, an image of exactly what you want. You have to know specifically what you desire, and vividly visualizing yourself as achieving that goal will actually help you attain it, but first you must know clearly what you seek. As Hill said, in setting out on a goal the first step is to *form a clear image in your mind of exactly what it is that you want.*

Now that you have that idea, Hill said that you must *write it down* in complete detail. Put your goals in writing!

After becoming clear about your goal and writing it down, next you must think it through and work it backwards to determine what sacrifices will be required to achieve it. What will you have to give in return to attain this? Is it time, money or some other type of resource? Will you need extra grit and determination to deal with the obstacles and hurdles you will surely face trying to bring it to life? What will you have to give in order to receive?

Hill said you must *create a list* of everything you will have to do in order to achieve your goal. Sometimes you can find someone else who has already achieved what you want and then, as the field of NLP (neuro-linguistic programming) suggests you can then simply model yourself on their process and behavior since it was already highly successful.

After you have all this down, you must next *create a plan* encompassing these steps, perhaps a sequential flowchart or map of the actions required to move you forward. *You must organize all the necessary steps into an action plan of achievement.*

Studies show that those who plan out the individual steps of the process required for achieving their goals produce far better outcomes than if they focused on either visualizing or just knowing the outcome they wanted. This is because thinking about the action steps you must take helps to focus your mind on the milestones to be passed and challenges you will realistically have to overcome to achieve your objective.

If you harbor an aspiration, you cannot simply remain at the stage of wishful imagination but must turn a dream into a sequence of to-do action steps that must be executed. If you cannot map out a procedure of execution to follow then you might not believe that your dream is actually possible, and if that's the case then you will have trouble rallying yourself to make the necessary efforts to work at it.

After you've done all this you must write out a clear, concise statement of what you want to achieve or acquire, the deadline or timeframe for its achievement, what you intend to give/do in return for it, and the actual plan for achievement that includes all your short-term sub-goals that lead to its fulfillment.

It is best to put this all in a notebook so that there is a readily available written record you can reference that helps you track your efforts at progress.

Everything in this plan must be specific, measurable and realistic (achievable, attainable) where neither the goals nor steps to be taken are too high, vague or unrealistic. The mind will rebel at expecting miracles so the steps you decide upon might stretch you, but they will have to be reasonable and realistic.

While Hill's advice was that you must set deadlines for all your goals, in some cases (such as goals that involve uncontrollable) it is better to set a schedule to operate by rather than a deadline for a task's completion.

If you cannot control various matters where you would normally want a deadline then it is better to drop the time table and simply *commit to a process* designed to consistently work towards your goal's achievement. With this type of situation you must schedule your process steps as situations permit. It is much easier and often more fruitful to commit to a process/system you will follow that lets results arise of themselves as they occur instead of insisting on a deadline when you cannot control the completion date of your efforts.

However, you can certainly schedule intentions that include specific dates and times, such as "I will do the following on this Date in this Place at this Time." Research reported in the *British Journal of Health Psychology* has shown that deciding in advance explicitly when and where you will take specific actions for achieving a goal can double or triple your chances for success. Once again we have the benefit of to-do lists since they accomplish this.

Basically, if you don't plan out your actions (as Napoleon Hill advises) you will be relying on a burning desire and willpower in order to always push forward. It is hard for people to continually keep up a degree of motivation without some assistance. However, if you explicitly plan where and when you must act you are much more likely to stick to accomplishing your goals and objectives. By sticking to a schedule you will find it much easier to achieve your goals because of the simple fact that you will do the action steps required.

The Magic of "Now"

After you have your goals and a plan, Hill advised that you start working on it immediately. Starting right away, even if you don't feel completely ready, is one of the keys to getting things done. There is no perfect time to start, so after having written things down you should make use of momentum and just start. When do you start? You just start *now!* As the Nike commercials proclaim, "Just do it!"

"Now" is the buzzword that reduces procrastination and the friction of starting. *Now* gets things done. In writing things down you have taken the first step of many necessary actions and deeds, rather than words, are what count. To show commitment to what is important to you, you must take action on your plan immediately, meaning now!

David Allen, in his book *Getting Things Done*, suggests a little productivity trick that can often help you use "now" to get things done. Called the "Two Minute Rule," you can use it in many areas of life. The rule is extremely simple: if it takes less than two minutes to do something then do it now. We put off an incredible number of things that take just two minutes or less so if it only takes two minutes to complete something then *do it now.*

All right, now that you have your goal and a plan of action, Napoleon Hill says that every day you should read your plan aloud, in the morning and at night (like a nightly review before bed) to refresh your motivations and original intentions that are bound to wane over time. By focusing at the start and end of each day, and tracking your progress with to-do lists and a journal, you will then stay focused on your goals and maintain productivity every day.

When reviewing your goals, you might even practice visualizing yourself already in possession of whatever you are seeking or spend some moments visualizing yourself going through the various stages of its accomplishment. Spending a few moments each day rehearsing the perfect outcome in your mind through mental imagery will definitely help you move through the change process more easily. Furthermore, visualizing the steps you must take will train your brain for success and help you prepare for the challenges you know must be faced.

Now you must resolve to do something every day that moves you towards your major goal. Remember that the system of to-do lists, regular reviews and larger goal setting periods can organize this so that it becomes automatic. They will help you with staying realistic with your efforts in that if you want something you may have to go through pain to get it. Therefore if you really want you are going to have to work for it in a systematic manner.

For instance, professional boxer Muhammad Ali did an interview with *Newsweek* in 1978 where he discussed his hard training and said, "I hated every minute of it. But I said to myself, 'Suffer now, and live the rest of your life as a champion.'" Louis Armstrong also commented, "Bleed the hours of your life, if your work is worth it."

Although Hill did not mention it, you also need to set up a system for periodically reviewing your goals as we have discussed, judging past actions and decisions by questions such as, "Does this task take me closer to my goals or not? Was this the best and highest use of my time?" We covered this when talking about spending one hour per week reviewing your past actions and making to-do lists of priority items help to insure that you are working on what matters.

You also need to set up an accounting feedback system that measures your progress and tracks your steps to see that you are staying on course for what you desire. Otherwise your intentions will wane, your motivation will wane and then your efforts will drop away like dust being dispersed by the wind.

Are you progressing toward your goals? Are you completing your action steps? Is what you are doing working, and if not then what isn't working? How can you change it?

If you continue doing the same thing that isn't working you are likely to continue getting the same results.

When Less is More

Along these lines you must remember the rule that it is often the things you stop doing that propel you ahead rather than the things you have been working on to move you forward. Progress is often made by subtracting away things that don't work rather than by adding on extra activities that you hope will move you ahead. That's the meaning of the mantra, "*Stop doing stupid things.*"

For instance, Japan went from a country known for producing low-quality goods to a powerhouse of industry and the second largest economy in the world. How did it do this? By teaching its manufacturers to adopt the quality control philosophy of William Edwards Deming to build better products that have higher quality because of fewer production process errors. The idea of "six sigma manufacturing" that caught on in the west also embodies this same notion.

Japanese companies therefore strove to improve their product quality through the *subtraction process* of eliminating mistakes and errors while western firms were focused on the *adding philosophy* of doing more of what worked to make products bigger, faster or more powerful. The Japanese chose the route of doing less of what doesn't work, and by avoiding stupid errors they leaped ahead.

When examining your process for achievement you

must always take these two possible paths (of addition or subtraction) into consideration. What can you do less of, what can you eliminate (in terms of habits or errors) that will help you achieve your goals easier? It is often what you stop doing that solves your problems rather than what you do more of to get better, such as increasing business profits by closing an unprofitable company division rather than by selling more products.

You can also clearly see the power of this strategy in the investment field where traders who learn to cut their losses usually make more money than those who don't. People who choose to lose weight by eating fewer sugar-laden foods also often achieve that goal without having to take the extra step of going to the gym.

If you just eliminate the weeds in your garden then the flowers might grow without need of any extra fertilizer, and this is something to remember when working towards your goals. Stop doing what isn't working. Stop doing stupid stuff that is distracting you away from what is the highest and best.

You must be a little bit introspective to discover those negative, harmful actions. Also, you might try to figure out how every action you want to undertake might be made a little bit more effective if you go about doing it in a better way.

Olympic Athletes and Deep Practice

In his wonderful book, *The Talent Code*, Daniel Coyle made the point that Olympic-level athletes and world class artists, musicians and other professionals are trying to achieve the goal of excellence and to do so they most often adhere to a schedule of what he termed deliberate, deep practice. The right type of deep practice can take someone of average abilities and turn them into an exceptional performer.

A person who pursues excellence should take any

skill/talent they wish to master (for us it would be a larger task we wish to accomplish), break it down into smaller chunk-sized pieces, and like the Japanese, practice to perform each of those component pieces with error-free perfection. Relying upon repetition, they must move out of their training comfort zone to a learning zone where they are practicing once again in a challenging way and where mastery at this new level will move them closer to excellence.

Skill is considered a form of memory, and so they must engage in vast amounts of training to build reliable neural brain circuits that constitute a pathway of skills without performance errors. They must devote themselves to deliberate efforts at improving their performance in all the component skills that make up a great performance. Visualization practice is supposed to help you with such efforts.

In deep practice you repeatedly train to master each component segment of a skill without errors, and then you must later link all these error-free performances together into a cohesive larger whole. Deliberately exaggerating a skill by changing the tempo (fastness or slowness) or magnitude (large and small) of execution can help you find and fix mistakes that would normally escape attention. Spotting and eliminating small errors to make each piece perfect is therefore part of the overall process for getting ahead.

People often overlook the fact that tiny things play a big role in the successful accomplishment of goals and getting things done. Usually we think that the secrets to success involve complicated mega-strategies or special techniques that only insiders know and practice. Winning UCLA basketball coach John Wooden (with eleven NCAA titles, twenty-five Final Four wins, four undefeated seasons, and countless winning streaks) – a great coach and leader - debunked that myth by teaching his players that small, basic tasks were the building blocks of winning games.

As an example of the importance of simplicity, on the first day of training Wooden would painstakingly instruct new recruits, in detail, how to put on their socks and shoes, a simple lesson most thought beneath them. Wooden would explain, "You see, if there are wrinkles in your socks or your shoes aren't tied properly, you will develop blisters. With blisters, you'll miss practice (playing time). If you miss practice you don't play. And if you don't play, we cannot win. If you want to win Championships, you must take care of the smallest of details."

The whole idea about deep practice for learning skills is not just about following a rigorous training schedule to push you forward, but practicing in a special way that involves the finding and fixing of even the smallest mistakes and errors that might derail you. This constant process of improvement by subtracting away errors, which we should also try to perform for our lives through our weekly one-hour reviews, will help you to quickly move ahead and get things done. If you are truly interested in mastering a skill or some other road of accomplishment then this is a topic you should investigate.

The whole quality control idea of eliminating errors, as practiced in Japanese production lines, and removing them from your process, as found in deep practice, is often what is necessary to produce Olympic level athletes. You can use this idea in your own goal setting and accomplishment efforts as well. Whether you improve a process by either addition or subtraction, the overarching goal is still that of optimization and incremental progress to move ahead.

Get Better By Improving a Little Bit Each Day

The practice of using daily to-do lists will move you forward in executing the tasks which have the most importance for your longer-term goals. Eliminating errors can become part of that overall process. The idea of getting better each day by going after marginal improvements, even if they aren't readily visible, can also have a tremendous impact on your life outcomes and the process of getting things done quicker and faster.

A story that amply illustrates the effectiveness of this approach concerns a winning turnaround in British cycling, which had only won a single gold medal in its decades-long history. The general manager of the British team, Sir Dave Brailsford, in 2002 took on the challenge of managing the team, and like the Japanese in their quality control efforts emphasized the process of tiny incremental improvements in order to score wins.

Brailsford reasoned that if he and his team broke down everything they could possibly think of that goes into competing on a racing bike, and then improved each element by 1%, they would then be able to achieve a significant increase in performance and start winning races. Therefore they searched for 1% marginal improvements in everything they did. They started optimizing training practices, the nutrition of the cyclists, the weight of the bicycle tires, and basically sought out 1% improvements everywhere.

As he explained in an interview with the *Harvard Business Review*, "By experimenting in a wind tunnel, we searched for small improvements to aerodynamics. By analyzing the mechanics area in the team truck, we discovered that dust was accumulating on the floor, undermining bike maintenance. So we painted the floor white, in order to spot any impurities. We hired a surgeon to teach our athletes about proper hand-washing so as to avoid illnesses during competition (we also decided not to shake any hands during the Olympics). We were precise about food preparation. We brought our own mattresses and pillows so our athletes could sleep in the same posture every night. We searched for small improvements everywhere and found countless opportunities. Taken together, we felt they gave us a competitive advantage."

Brailsford explained that they experienced some failures when they lost sight of the larger picture in their push at micro-optimizations. "We tried so hard with all the bells and whistles of marginal gains that our focus was too much on the periphery and not on the core. You have to identify the critical success factors and ensure they are in place, and then focus your improvements around them. That was a harsh lesson."

However, once on track the strategy eventually triumphed because British cyclists won gold medals at the 2008 London Olympics, gold medals at the 2012 London Olympics, and multiple wins in the Tour de France. This shows the power of continuous process improvement achieved by tiny incremental gains due to eliminating errors.

I can think of many cases in business where the idea of breaking long processes into smaller component pieces, and then optimizing each step of these processes (such as by *benchmarking* for best practices), can produce big changes in a firm's profitability and productivity.

When you look at every single system within a company – how you answer the telephone, how you open the mail, how you file papers, how you do your bookkeeping, accounting, purchasing and marketing, etcetera – you can always tear it apart and analyze, "Why are we doing it that way? Is there a better way to do it? Who is doing this better that we can copy?"

Most people never ask those benchmarking questions. They just keep on doing what it is that they have always done without question, and in doing the same things in the same ways without ever trying to improve matters they never seem to get ahead.

Can you use this new philosophy in life? Yes, and you also have the principles for creating a uniquely effective performance program.

5
Yearly Goal Setting

Daily to-do lists which focus on task priorities, and weekly review sessions to help you work better on your objectives will together move you towards your goals. However, for help in accomplishing the largest goals you will need an outlook that is greater in scope than that provided by just daily or weekly efforts. For that you need monthly and yearly goal setting methods, as Frank McKinney has clearly illustrated. I personally use the following method to do this.

Every year before January 1, I buy a new notebook for that year which will contain my yearly, monthly and life goals and objectives that I redo each year. Some people might call my small notebook a "yearly journal" since I also use it to jot down significant events and insights during the year when they occur, and so it also serves as a record of useful memories.

My collection of these small notebooks goes back decades and each yearly notebook has within it all the significant things I have accomplished and worked on (as well as special insights I have learned) during every month of that year. It is great to be able to look back at any month in any year and see what activities I was pursuing at that time (such as going to see a certain movie, taking a trip or buying something of significance). The notebooks contain monthly to-do lists that reflect my yearly goals as well as various other activities that I wanted to accomplish during each month.

Here is how I create this annual goal setting (and achievement) journal every year.

Every year I go through an exercise where I think about my bigger life goals and then put down whatever I have decided on the back pages of the new annual journal. I will walk you through the process of how to create a list of these life goals in a moment, but for now I just want to say that the conclusion of that yearly exercise always goes on the last page of the notebook.

It is interesting that I can easily glance back at the last pages of previous journals and see how my goals, dreams, and aspirations have changed over the years. This is bound to happen for you, too.

On the first page of the yearly journal I make a list of all the major goals or activities that I want to accomplish or experience for that year. This includes anything from major trips I want to take, items I want to purchase, how much money I want to save, and things I might want to do such as take a course on scuba diving.

The yearly goals list will include both major and minor items with the one commonality being that they are all the things I wish to do or experience that year and I also agree to push myself to accomplish those things *that year*. Throughout the year I periodically look at this front page of goals for the year to refresh my motivation for achieving those targets, and that periodic review actually helps me force myself to accomplish them.

The rest of the book contains sections for each month of the year, which I fill in with monthly goals and activities when every new month arises. When each month arrives I immediately label a new page "January," "February," "March," "April" and so on. Next I list the goals I wish to accomplish in that specific month.

Many of the activities I list have nothing to do with my major goals for that year or life in general. They are just things I want to do that month such as get a checkup from the doctor, read a book I always wanted to read, buy some new shirts, see a movie, contact some old friends and so forth. The monthly list is a great way of making sure you do things you know you should or would like to do, but which because of lethargy, procrastination or the effort required you are more than likely to put off.

In other words, writing down your goals at the beginning of the month and reviewing this on a daily basis during the month will make it more likely that you will schedule them into to-do lists and actually do them. Naturally, as soon as I complete a goal I cross it off my list of to-dos for the month.

Many long-term goals you have might be far too big to actually accomplish in one gulp. If a task is really big then its sheer size might scare you from taking any required action, so you must chop up big tasks into several smaller tasks in order to be able to complete them. Many of those tasks will wind up on the monthly to-do lists within this journal.

Basically, large goals almost always have to be broken down into smaller sub-goals so that you can maintain the motivation and effort necessary to accomplish them. After all, short-term sub-goals that can be accomplished in thirty days are far more likely to be achieved than longer-term goals that might take years.

Now as important things of significance happen in a month, or as I read books or websites and learn something important, I also jot down those notables in my yearly journal. This is how I slowly build up a track record of what I was thinking and doing for the year.

Writing down my insights, lessons learned, mistakes

not to be repeated, actions, turning points and so on has helped me become a better and more productive person. As Benjamin Franklin said when he commented upon his own ledgering method for self-improvement, "I have had the personal satisfaction of seeing errors gradually diminish due to this technique and have become a better and happier man than otherwise I would have been had I not used this method."

My yearly journals have become a life management system for proactive planning and prioritizing. You can use this same system – and I do urge you to emulate it in some way - to extend into all areas of your life to make it richer and better on every level ... physical, emotional, mental and spiritual. It represents a solid way of turning your dreams into actions that will move you to your higher calling and what you actually want to achieve, experience and accomplish in life.

The Life Goals Exercise

As mentioned, each year I go through a little exercise to re-determine my life goals, which sometimes change because of different priorities. One of the exercises I annually run through was taught to me by a famous motivational influence expert, and I always put its results on the last few pages of my yearly journal. It only takes a few minutes to carry out his goal setting technique so I advise you to follow along as you are reading. Afterwards we will go over an alternative method as well - which is the one most people prefer - but you really need to know both methods.

My famous friend said that the best way to determine worthy goals for your life is to start with a clean sheet of paper and make four squares on it. Give each of the squares one of the following labels: "Health," "Business-Career-Wealth," "Intellectual Life," and "Spiritual Life."

Next, start writing down all your goals, dreams and

desires that you have in each of the relevant squares. Make a list of everything you want to have, do, own or experience for each of these categories and write down items in the relevant boxes. This should only take a few minutes.

Now comes the difficult part. For each item on a list you must now write down the *reason you must have that goal.* If there aren't any reasons then cross off that item because that wish or desire is just a whim. If you cannot think of a good reason why you must attain/experience that goal then it isn't worth your efforts as compared to something else which has definite reasons.

You must also write down the pain you will feel if you *don't* achieve that target along with the pleasure you will feel if you do achieve it. Those items that have both a pain factor and pleasure factor are probably the ones that will carry the most significance for you. If you won't feel both pleasure at achieving something and pain if you do not then you will probably never generate the commitment required to attain it.

A famous stock trader once explained to me the importance of acknowledging pain when setting goals. He said that that the reason he became successful at trading, whereas most people fail, was not just because he wanted it badly but because there was a pain to not achieving the success he wanted, and that pain helped motivate him to finally succeed after a long string of failures. As a student of psychology, he explained that someone who loves winning but also hates losing is far more motivated and likely to win than someone who just loves winning or just hates losing. He explained that you needed the emotions of both pain and pleasure to motivate yourself towards achieving difficult goals.

Harkening back to Gail Matthews' study on goal setting, you might reason that the individuals in her study who sent updates to their supportive friends about their progress would feel embarrassed if they stopped working towards the goals they had publicly announced, and so the pain of not completing a goal has to be factored in as a positive motivator. Fear or embarrassment can be strong motivators to success, and this exercise simply weeds out those goals that don't have any strong emotional components attached to them.

Unless success just naturally happens for you, the goals you are likely to achieve in life probably have both a pain and pleasure component to their accomplishment and in this exercise you are determining which goals have the strongest motivations. Those are the ones that should probably be your top priorities.

Finally, with your four boxes filled up with desires/goals and with all the priorities now determined you can next work on identifying the action steps needed to complete these goals and get you to where you want to go.

Just as Napoleon Hill advised, you must realistically recognize that obstacles might stand in the way of everything you want, so it will be useful to break the goal achievement process into steps with deadlines. Do this for each of the important goals or dreams that you still think are important after doing the previous exercise. Now you know what is important to you, and what you have to do to achieve those outcomes.

Every year you need to go through this exercise and record your final set of life goals and action steps in your yearly goals notebook. Afterwards you can create yearly and monthly sub-goals from your decisions and set up some system that helps you consistently work towards their achievement.

This is an exercise that I do once every year, but since this refers to *life goals* I put it at the back of my annual goals journal. The front of my yearly journal is occupied by the annual goals to accomplish (things I want to do) that particular year while the middle of the notebook, as explained, contains the goals, activities desired and to-do lists for each month of the year. Every month I simply create a new page in the journal with a list of things I want or need to do that month, and then periodically review it as the month progresses so that I am always working towards completing those items.

When running through this annual goal-setting exercise, which I usually do the last week of each year, I also take the time to re-examine some higher philosophical issues such as whether I am pursuing the core values of my life in everything I am doing. You, too, should do this at the end of the year. I take a good look at myself and ask whether I'm living a balanced life, working to make the world a better place, setting higher standards for myself, being honest with my relationships, learning to be more perseverant, and being a constant learner. Am I basically living my life with integrity?

Every year I also re-evaluate my life goals by using a totally different exercise. This is the method I usually teach people at seminars, which is an exercise that can usually be completed in ten minutes or less.

Make a Bucket List

For this exercise you are going to make a list called "Life Goals" that is like a bucket list of "The Things I want to do before I die." You are about to make a list of everything you want to do or experience in this life time that has top priority or ultimate importance.

You must know exactly what you want your future to look like if you want to create it, and this exercise will help you arrive at that picture. While it is true that you may never get there since you can only control your personal actions and not the results of those actions, you will still have to go through the *process* of trying to create a new future since that is the only road that might get you there.

Since that road will involve your devoted energy and effort you must make sure your goals are worthy of you.

Therefore I want you to make a big list of whatever you still want to experience in life, everything great and small, and then we will weed out what isn't important.

First, we have to get everything down on paper, so at the back of your yearly journal I want you to write down your life goals and the things you might like to experience and accomplish in life. This will include activities great and small like learning how to dance, creating a blog, eating at a particular restaurant, visiting special places, toys you would like to own, skills you want to acquire and events you want to experience.

Write down whatever you want to do in life as a goal or aspiration. Here are some questions you can ask yourself that will help you complete this step. What do you want your life to look like? What do you want to have or experience? What do you want to achieve? What do you want people to write on your tombstone? What is your desired destination?

For instance, what five things would give you the greatest sense of accomplishment in your *personal life*? What five things do you want to achieve that would give you a great sense of accomplishment in your *business life*? How much money do you want to be making? How much in assets do you want to accumulate before retirement? What type of house would you like to be living in? What ten places would you like to visit? What five skills would you most want to acquire? What five toys would you most like to own? What would you like your family to experience over the next five years?

Think about what makes you happy and filled with excitement. What would make your life richer or give you a feeling of being filled with purpose? What do you enjoy doing and what are your obsessions? What are you constantly returning to think about time and again? What would you enjoy doing the rest of your life? What would you really want to do with your time even if it doesn't pay you money?

Make a list of everything you want to do, own, learn, share, experience and so on. Keep writing until you are done and try to make as comprehensive a list as possible. It can fill pages if you like, but truth be told most people can finish this type of list in well under ten minutes. They usually don't even need to sleep on it.

Once done, look at your list. It might have twenty, thirty or forty items on it. For the next step of the process you will narrow it down to just your *top ten choices.* Cross off everything on your list except the top ten most important items.

Once you have cut the list to just ten items, pause and think for a while about what remains, and then go back and cut the list down to *just your top four or five goals.*

My famous friend told me studies show that if you have not done these four or five things yet and you are over thirty years of age then *there is an 80% chance you won't finish them unless you do this exercise!*

Imagine that! You probably won't achieve or experience the most important four or five things you want in this life if you don't write them down and then create a goals system to accomplish them.

You can now understand why I always tell people to do this exercise on a yearly basis. You want this life to count. You want your actions to matter. If there is anything you should shoot for it should be the four or five things that you really want out of life! You already decided that life would be better if you achieved these goals so go after them.

It is time now to convert those goals into five-year plans of achievement. Give yourself no more than five years to complete each of these four (or five) major life items. Figure out when you will be working on what and if some objectives can be started right away or have to be tabled until later.

Next, create one year lists and then monthly lists from those five-year plans. From a monthly list you can create weekly lists and then daily to-do lists just as has been explained.

You now have all the pieces that you can put everything together into one single coordinated system. Life goals, yearly goals, monthly, weekly and daily goals can all be brought together into one cohesive, proactive goals-setting and accomplishment system.

How do you break larger objectives into smaller ones? Well, someone who wants to save $1,200 this year might turn this into a sub-goal of saving $100 per month. Someone who wants to lose weight might turn this into a target of losing a certain number of pounds each month. Better yet, they might turn it into a goal of eating one less wheat item per day (such as a morning bagel, afternoon pastry, or dinner desert) and refraining from all soft drinks and sugar laden beverages on a daily basis.

Remember that what you have identified through this exercise are *your* priorities, *your* dreams, *your* visions, *your* interests. They belong to you and no one else. You will have to sacrifice lesser interests to achieve them, but these are your dreams for your life. They are what is important to you, what you want to achieve, do and experience after much soul searching. This is what you want out of life. These are your highest aspirations!

Because you have thought through them and even sketched out a blueprint of the steps necessary for their accomplishment, you now have a much better chance to achieve these dreams (that you deem the most important to your life) than if you never did these exercises at all. Furthermore, having gone through these exercises, you also now know what are your highest priorities in life.

Putting It All Together

One man who mastered this particular goal setting technique and the act of putting it all together is the famous entrepreneur and management expert Michael

Masterson. *In Automatic Wealth for Grads* he explained how he does this type of exercise in his own unique way, which you might also care to follow. He writes:

"Whether you're an optimist, a pessimist, or something between, recognize that whatever your goals are, you'll have a better chance of achieving them if you follow a formal goal-setting program.

"So let's set up your program right now. Take out a sheet of paper. Title it 'Life's Goals' (if you have no shame) or 'Stuff to Do Before I Croak' (if you are afraid someone will see it.

"Now make a list of everything you want to accomplish. Everything. Making a lot of money. Writing books. Traveling to Rome. Learning to tap dance. Write till you are done.

"Let the list sit for a few hours—even a day. Then narrow it down to your top 10 choices. Then take another rest. Now make another cut. This time, you have to select your top four goals.

"Okay, these are your life goals, top priorities, bottom-line objectives.

"Now, of the four, pick one that is numero uno. On a separate sheet of paper-or perhaps on an index card—write down your four goals with your number one objective on top. Highlight that one.

"Convert those four goals into five-year objectives. For example, let's say that one of your life goals is to have a net worth of $10 million. And let's say you want to retire in 10 years. You might make 'having a $5 million net worth' your five-year goal.

"You are going to use this five-year list to create a one-year list. And you will use the one-year list to create monthly lists. And you will use each monthly list to create weekly lists. And the weekly lists to create daily task lists.

"I know. I know. But it works. It really works.

"If you make these four goals your priorities, you will almost surely have to sacrifice other, lesser objectives to achieve them. And to make sure you reach your top goal, you may even have to compromise one or more of the other three. But by using this plan, you will definitely achieve that primary goal—and you will have a much better chance of accomplishing the other three than you would ever have had otherwise.

"How will you find the time in your already busy schedule to do what you have to do to reach your life goals? It's easy to do so: Wake up—and get to work— earlier. And use that extra time to do the things that matter most in terms of your long term success.

"Every successful businessman I know (or have read about) gets to work early. It's such a universal trait of accomplished individuals that I'm tempted to say it is a secret for success. 'Early to bed and early to rise,' Ben Franklin said, 'makes a man healthy, wealthy and wise.' I used to think that was propaganda from a Puritan. Now I think it's an observation from a very wise man.

"Think of it this way:

"Somewhere inside you a fire is burning. It is your core desire—your desire—your deepest, truest idea about what you'd like to do and the person you'd like to become. If you can vent that fire, it will give you all the energy, imagination, and boldness you need to make your life full, rich, and satisfying. If you ignore that fire, it will consume everything that is potentially great and good about you. It will burn out your secret hopes, desires, and passions, one at a time, and leave you – as an older person reflecting back on your life – with a cold, charred core.

"By getting up early each morning and making those early hours – as well as the rest of your day – more productive, you can make your life into exactly what it should be. What it should be, of course, is different for every person. Only by digging down deep and finding out what really motivates you – by identifying your life goals – can you find the fire that will fuel your future."

Michael Masterson thus showed how to turn larger

goals into smaller objectives and linked everything together all the way down to the habit of getting up earlier so that he might find extra time per day to accomplish all his aspirations.

If you want to accomplish big things in life, you must learn how to prioritize the activities of your life. Furthermore, you must cut out whatever is non-essential if it distracts you from your goals. Then you must set up some systematic method of accomplishment that takes into account your normal daily, weekly, monthly and yearly schedules.

As Briana Scurry (two time Olympic gold medal champion for women's soccer) explained about judging the importance of activities, "About six months before an Olympics, I would relate all the decisions I made to the ultimate vision of winning gold. The simple question I would ask several times a day was, 'Will this activity help me perform better and therefore help us win gold?' This question guided me in the right direction. Even if the activity was taking the day off or stepping back for a bit to get better perspective, being mindful of that vision helped me choose the best course of action in order to achieve the goal."

You should most certainly cut out distractions and concentrate foremost on achieving the goals and aspirations that are most important to you in life. Do you really want to achieve those goals, or would you rather put your time into activities of lesser importance?

These two exercises help you get started on determining what is really important to you, yet there is one more I'd like to introduce that comes from the billionaire Warren Buffett.

Warren Buffett's Method

Warren Buffett is a brilliant investor who uses a different system to come up with priorities that he revealed when helping his personal airplane pilot determine career his priorities. Buffett asked Mike Flint, his pilot, to go through a three-step priorities exercise as follows.

First, Buffett explained to Flint, you have to write down your top twenty-five career goals, which Flint easily did. Next, Buffett asked Flint to circle his top five goals out of this list.

This left Flint with two lists ... a list of five items that were his primary focus and a list of other items that came in close. When Buffett asked Flint what he thought about those uncircled items, Flint explained that since they came in close second they were still important so he would work on achieving them intermittently as he saw fit.

Buffett replied, "No, you've got it wrong. What you didn't circle just became your list of goals to avoid working on at all costs. No matter what, these things should get none of your attention until you have succeeded in achieving your top five."

Once again we find a goal setting lesson on the importance and power of setting priorities and just focusing on accomplishing those things which are most important. If you focus on working at those goals that have the highest priority in your life then you are sure to move ahead. If you don't because you work on everything of interest then it will be difficult to accomplish the greatest goals of your life.

Don't dilute your energy and attention by working on many things of interest. Focus on accomplishing only the ones with highest priority, the ones that will get you to where you want to go.

6
The Eight M's

The last step to this whole process is the actual physical, do-it-yourself march towards accomplishment. As we are talking about goal setting, productivity and time management, I always tell people that they need *Four M's* in order to proactively change their life for the better and/or achieve something of significance in life. I call these the "Material M's." If people are spiritually inclined then I add another set of Four M's, the "Spiritual M's," to make *Eight M's* in total.

The initial Four M's summarize the ingredients necessary for getting things done in a quick and efficient manner. They encompass or encapsulate the typical mundane road of success and accomplishment.

If you don't bring these Four M's into your life then you will probably just drift along with the winds of fate and have to accept whatever life brings you because you won't actively create what you want. By choice you won't be actively building a future you desire, but will just be passively accepting, for good or bad, whatever comes your way.

I would rather people learn how to seize life and make it into what they want rather than let the "winds of karma" simply push them around. I want people to feel that they can become brave sailors who can chart a course to lands unvisited and handle whatever winds blow against them.

The Material M's

The **First M** you need in order to achieve a goal in business or life is Motivation, or the passion and strong desire to change things for the better. You cannot just magically attract success to yourself through some hocus-pocus type of manifestation that just involves wishful thinking. You must *make* things happen, and to do that you need a level of desire, inspiration and motivation that is strong enough to keep you working on creating that new future.

Motivation is the spark of ignition that initially gets things going and which also keeps you moving forward. Without sufficient motivation the entire process of accomplishment will never ignite and never be completed.

Don't expect that you can just wish something into manifestation as people claimed in *The Secret*. You need work to create a new future, a new life. It is not enough just to think it; you need to act and to act you need motivation to power you forward.

The **Second M** that one needs is a Model, Method or Master plan of action for accomplishing that change you desire. The fastest way to do that is to find other successful people and model (copy) them for the progress steps you need to make. You model the successful masters who are already the best at it by finding out exactly what they did to get that way, and then do the same things.

You definitely need a method to achieve any great objective. You need a systematic plan involving daily, weekly or monthly disciplined effort, i.e. what we have covered in the earlier chapters. You need a plan of directions for getting to where you want to go and then you must align yourself with this plan of action for success.

Once the motivation and plan are ready, the **Third M** that you need is to actually start Moving forward with Massive intelligent action. Now is the time to work smart and work hard. As Napoleon Hill said, immediately start moving forward after you have made your plans even if you don't feel absolutely ready. You need to employ massive, intelligent and disciplined action in pursuit of your desired destination once you decide what it is.

Once started, you will need to keep the momentum (progress) going, which usually requires some type of management method to ensure that you keep on a road of effective action until your goal is accomplished. You ultimately need perseverance and grit to keep pursuing your target, which requires some type of management system to keep you marching forward on track. Without some management system that keeps you locked on target and moving in that direction, you are likely to be defeated by feelings such as boredom, frustration, or even indifference that are likely to arise along any long path to success.

The **Fourth M** is that you need a Monitoring system to measure your progress at advancement and keep you on track to your desired destination. You should track your progress using a feedback system that compares how you are doing with what is expected. A measuring system (such as a monthly ledgering journal) will keep record of the progress you make and milestones you accomplish, and by frequently reviewing it you will be able to spot when you are off target. As Ernest Hemingway said, "Keep track of your output - kidding yourself is for amateurs."

Are you staying on course or drifting off course? Are you getting closer to your goals or moving farther away?

Are you achieving the sub-goals and tasks you set for yourself? Are you making errors in execution?

You already have the basics of such a monitoring system with your daily to-do lists, weekly review sessions or problem solving workshops, your monthly and quarterly meetings, and your yearly goal setting and life purpose exercises. These create an interlocked system of components you can pick and choose from in order to help you move ahead towards your aspirations.

Even so, as you start marching forward you also need some way to judge how you are progressing against some type of standard that is relevant to your final goals and objectives. You need a fair barometer to tell you how you are doing, and to help you determine what is and isn't working in your approach. This standard might be the typical expectations for the task, a perfect model of performance you judge yourself against, the best known performance in the field or your personal best at the task.

The purpose of monitoring your progress is so that you can produce some form of adjustment when you are falling behind or drifting off target. You have to find the errors in your performance and then, rather than blame others, take responsibility for those errors, correct them and alter the way you act.

Whenever you try to do something you must be flexible and willing to change what you are doing if things are not going according to plan and you are not getting the results you hope for. If you continue doing the same thing when veering off course then you cannot expect any different results from what you are already getting. If you are unwilling to adjust your ways after going astray then you are also in danger of achieving nothing.

That's just life in general! If you continue doing the same things in life then you'll just get the same results. If what you are doing isn't taking you to where you want then you just have to change. If you want change, any type of change, you have to do something new.

These Four M's actually summarize the basic western path of goal setting and achievement. Whether you talk about the methods of Napoleon Hill, Brian Tracy, Clement Stone or others they will commonly say that you need motivation, method, massive intelligent action and then a monitoring system to keep you on track to achieving your goals and desires.

To this I will only add what Aristotle said nearly two thousand years ago that actually summarizes the Napoleon Hill method: "First, have a definite, clear, practical ideal; a goal, an objective. Second, have the necessary means to achieve your ends: wisdom, money, materials, and methods. Third, adjust all your means to that end."

The Spiritual M's

Few westerners know that there is an eastern counterpart to the western path of attainment which adds four more M's to this basic list. Then we have the Eight M's in total.

Rather than having a materialistic slant, each of the four eastern M's deals with a spiritual force that may help you with goal achievement. In other words, eastern spiritual traditions commonly advocate four additional M's that encapsulate the dimension of spiritual assistance available to you that you can tap into for attaining your goals.

The **First Spiritual M** here is that someone who wants to achieve various goals or accomplish particular deeds in life needs to practice Meditation. Meditation is the first M from the east.

Most people have unclear minds, and don't take stock of what they are doing or thinking in the moment. They are not mindful of their thoughts. Meditation is the cultivation of clear present awareness - you cultivate a mind of clarity that can perfectly know all the thoughts and emotions that arise within it as they appear. You don't suppress thoughts but practice detachment from thoughts so that you always let them be born, but never cling to them or hold them longer than is necessary. So if you are sad you are sad, and when it is over you don't try to keep clinging to sadness. This is what is called freedom of the mind; it is not the fact that sadness never arrives!

During meditation you practice watching your thoughts like an independent third person observer. This is called witnessing. By observing your thoughts without attachment (mindfulness) you become *clearly* and unabashedly aware of your mind's doings. Through meditation practice, you learn self-awareness and how to concentrate. In particular, you especially learn how to maintain in-the-moment-awareness of whatever you are thinking and doing.

That practice of watching your thoughts to you're your own thoughts perfectly know what you are thinking and doing, without losing yourself in your thoughts or getting carried away by your behavior, enables you to correct any errant thoughts and actions that might move you away from accomplishing a specific goal you want.

That's the importance of meditation - it helps you cultivate a mind of clear awareness through which you can more easily monitor your own actions and behavior. By cultivating a state of clear presence where you know your own mind, that's how you can get a handle on changing your behavior and then change your life and fortune for the better. The best performers in many fields are known to observe themselves closely, and are able to step outside of themselves to monitor what is in their own minds.

Science calls this metacognition, where you are able to have knowledge of your own thinking, whereas many spiritual traditions just call this awareness. Awareness of your mind (your thoughts) is a key element in the pursuit of excellence and self-perfection. It is a key requirement for the field of accomplishments.

If you cultivate a mind of clarity that can focus, concentrate and stay on track without being bothered or sidetracked by wandering nuisance thoughts of no priority, and which can see all the thoughts within itself, then you'll have the ability to recognize errant thoughts whenever they arise and cut therefore them off before they interfere with your best efforts. Awareness (or metacognition) also helps you spot opportunities in evolving situations, such as when you are working towards your goals or life objectives, that can be used to your own benefit.

The **Second Spiritual M** from the east is that it is beneficial to have an enlightened Master. A master is like a wise coach or guide who can help you change your life in the way you want so that you can achieve the goals you are seeking. For instance, there are countless Chinese stories of the wise advice given by Zen masters to people who were trying to figure out how to accomplish some great deed, and Tibetan as well as Indian stories also abound as to the effectiveness of the advice of a highly developed spiritual guru. There are untold benefits to asking an enlightened spiritual sage, saint, master or guru for help or advice.

This brings up the **Third Spiritual M**, which is that anyone who wishes to achieve truly great things needs Merit for that attainment. Merit is the karmic reward you receive from doing kind acts and charitable deeds for others. The correct use of your behavior in personal and business life is said to earn you merit (good karma) whereas bad luck, bad results and bad fortune come from abandoning the road of virtue, morality and ethics in your thoughts and doings. Destiny and fate are thought to depend on your personal conduct and the right or wrong use of your thoughts and deeds.

For instance, someone in the business field whose product or service satisfies customers' needs and desires and who develops a reputation for honesty, quality, service and fair dealings will eventually win the award of higher sales and profits. They can become rich due to their "virtues," which is a worldly example of the merit achieved because of the correct ways of being and doing.

Westerners usually just say that "character is destiny" to capture this same idea, but the principle that good deeds will win you fortunate rewards is the principle of creating and accumulating merit for good fortune.

The last or **Fourth Spiritual M** from the east stands for Mantra, which the practice of asking for help from higher beings to achieve a goal. A mantra is a special phrase that you repeat just like a prayer. In the west, reciting prayers is a well-accepted practice of asking for heavenly help, and its equivalent in most eastern religions is the practice of reciting mantras.

We could say that the western practice of repeatedly using affirmations to support your goals and efforts is also a form of mantra practice. Since visualizations usually accompany many mantra practices, using visualizations together with mantras and/or affirmations can help support the accomplishment of your efforts and goals.

While many westerners believe that this set of Four M's represent superstitions, the ideas and principles behind them are greatly discussed in eastern classics like *Liao Fan's Four Lessons*. This book, which focuses on how someone can change their behavior in order to alter their fate, fortune and destiny, is so popular that it has spawned countless copycat versions over many centuries. It has had a tremendous influence on Asian culture and is one of the few books that I recommend parents introduce to their children.

Most Asian religions believe in karma, fate and fortunes (Hinduism, Buddhism, Taoism, Jainism, etc.). According to karmic thinking, what you have now in life or are due to receive in the future is to some extent fated because it is a reward from your past actions.

However, if you don't have something yet in life or have not yet experienced it then that goal can certainly be accomplished; it is not fated that you cannot enjoy or achieve something simply because you don't already have it and it is not indicated in your fortune. Many things are possible if you but work smartly to achieve them. What will help you achieve your goals and desires are the Four M's of the west along with the Four M's of the east that add spiritual power to your efforts.

The highest eastern view on fates and fortunes is that if the present self-effort towards a goal are sometimes thwarted by obstacles – which you might term "fate" - it simply means that your present self-effort is weak. This is why you need to consistently keep to a goals achievement system.

While many eastern religions recognize the existence of karma and fate, they also say that it is you who have created it. Therefore, as the author of your fate you, once again, have the power to change it. You have the ability to alter your life, change your fate and fortune, create something new, and achieve your goals and objectives. This, however, will take energy and smart effort. Any desire or pathway that goes against fate will require more than just the Four M's of the west. It will require the addition of the Four M's from the east!

It is simply ignorance to say that all life events are fated and therefore you should never push to try to uplift your life such as trying to change your living circumstances for the better. Easterners say that your actions may move along the lines that karma traces for you, but you also have free will that allows you to fashion your karma and achieve the goals you desire through the wise application of your will and efforts.

Basically, a life of awareness and wise actions guided by a strong will does not have to follow any preordained pattern. It can always achieve outcomes in excess of what fate had intended.

Therefore, if you want to achieve a goal or objective in excess of what is considered your fate, it is indeed possible. You can achieve goals that are not already "fated" in a life's fortune. You just need a system that harnesses your will as has already been delivered.

Easterners maintain that *there definitely is* such a thing as fate or karma. They say that it does exist and can at times be predicted. However, spiritual gurus commonly lament that most people just unknowingly go along with it because they cannot detach from the habits, impulses and inclinations that (karmically) impel them along the fated pathways they have already created. This is why you need meditation to be able to know your thoughts clearly and go against impulses that might send you down a fate you don't desire.

The way of defying fate and triumphing over habitual impulses is through a daily, weekly, monthly and yearly set of to-do lists for achieving important goals and objectives. By wedding yourself to a disciplined system of achievement that has a monitoring feedback mechanism that keeps you on track, you can cut across the lines of karma to indeed change fate and fortune and achieve a life you desire.

To create a new fortune or achieve some grand objective, easterners say the best means is to start with a clearly visualized goal that you want to achieve. Hence you have already been taught about the power of mental imagery and visualization.

Next you need to cultivate awareness, via the practice of meditation, so that your mind is always clear and can in real time see and then correct your own faults and errors (in thought and deed) that might veer you off course from achieving desired outcomes.

You can also ask an enlightened teacher to help you with your efforts or recite mantras asking for heavenly assistance, and these four extras are considered the reliable spiritual assists to the best models of achievement.

The western goal achievement method is to make a commitment, make a plan and then consistently apply yourself to a massive amount of intelligent action to achieve that goal. You will also need to be flexible and adjust yourself when going wrong, which requires a monitoring system that keeps you on course until completion.

Thus you can use the typical western method of goal achievement to achieve your goals in life, but if you feel something is missing and want to add an extra "umph" to your efforts then you must also consider adding the eastern methods of spiritual dimensions into your efforts.

There are the Four M's of the west and Four M's of the east for a total of Eight M's which you can call upon for getting things done.

7
Service to Humanity Versus Profits

There you have it – an integrated method for time management, productivity and accomplishing many things quickly by keeping to a course of actions you carefully schedule. You have a variety of methods for setting goals, overcoming the procrastination that blocks you from achieving them, accomplishing things quickly and getting things done.

Most people will use these methods for business and the pursuit of profits, but in parting I would like to leave you with just a simple thought which you might power whenever appropriate.

This is the idea that your business can be about something more than just the pursuit of profits. While pursuing profits and gainful employment, you can certainly be wed to a higher set of ethics and values. Your business career can also be about a higher mission and calling.

As seen in the story of the three masons building the cathedral, if you view your business through the lens of a higher calling then that new viewpoint and directive can totally transform the way you operate. It can even bring you more money.

Instead of thinking solely about profits and money, you might recast your objectives to consider how you might be the most useful to others. By becoming indispensable or offering the most service you will thereby, in return, be rewarded with more money or profits for the service you provide. And, if you focus on how you might give more without extra cost, this change in mindset might be the very thing that leads to a profitable breakthrough you are looking for.

A higher mission always entails being of better service to others, which actually is often more profitable since servicing people and solving their problems is a type of merit that must earn a reward. In the business realm, it is only by satisfying consumer needs and desires, which is a type of merit (offering service to others), that you can earn profits in the first place.

Unfortunately, most businessmen simply seek profits without any higher mission in their mind (or higher ethics either) and then losing sight of their morals do shameful things for a dollar. A famous story from ancient China reminds us of what happens when people lose sight of higher values and only think about monetary gain rather than righteousness.

The Story of Mencius

In D.C. Lau's translation of *Mencius* the story goes that the Chinese sage Mencius traveled a thousand miles to visit King Hui of Liang, and the king greeted him saying that he must have come because of some ideas for profiting his state.

Mencius rebuked him saying, "Your majesty, ... What is the point of mentioning the word 'profit'? All that matters is that there should be benevolence and rightness. If Your Majesty says, 'How can I profit my state?' and the Counselors say, 'How can I profit my family?' and the

Gentlemen and Commoners say, 'How can I profit my person?' then those above and those below will be trying to profit at the expense of one another and the state will be imperiled. When regicide is committed in a state of ten thousand chariots, it is certain to be by a vassal with a thousand chariots, and when it is committed in a state of a thousand chariots, it is certain to be by a vassal with a hundred chariots. A share of a thousand in ten thousand or a hundred in a thousand is by no means insignificant, yet if profit is put before rightness, there is no satisfaction short of total usurpation. No benevolent man ever abandons his parents, and no dutiful man ever puts his prince last. Perhaps you will now endorse what I have said, 'All that matters is that there should be benevolence and rightness. What is the point of mentioning the word "profit"?'"

Mencius pointed out the negative cascading effect on an entire nation when its people start focusing primarily on the goal of money (profits) rather than insisting on the principles of propriety, justice, virtue, correctness and righteousness in life. Character is indeed destiny. The moral fiber of a nation, and its focus on rightness and justice rather than profits, should take precedence over all else because everything will follow from the nation's core system of values.

If it sinks into people's consciousness that life is primarily about the pursuit of profit, and that it is fine to ignore correctness and do whatever is "lawful" regardless of virtue and righteousness, then a society is done for.

A Second Story

A second story, again from Chinese history, actually refers to this first story and adds flavor to the discussion. Found in Nan Huai-chin's *The Story of Chinese Zen*, it concerns the Grand Historian of China, Sima Qian, who upon reading this first story put down his book and sighed when he came to the place where King Hui of Liang asked Mencius, "How will you profit my country?"

At that point the Grand Historian said, "Ah, profit is truly the beginning of disorder. That is why Confucius seldom spoke of profit, always shoring up the source. The source is the beginning. Whether it is found among the upper classes or the lower classes, the degeneracy of lust for profit is basically the same. When those in public office profit unfairly, then the law is disordered. When those in the private sector profit by deception, then business is disordered. When business is disorderly, people are contentious and dissatisfied; when law is disorderly, the citizenry is resentful and disobedient. This is how people get to be so rebellious and belligerent that they don't care if they die. Is this not a demonstration of how, 'Profit is truly the beginning of disorder'? The sages and saints were deeply cautious and aloof from profit, giving honor and precedence to humanity and justice. But in later times there were still those who deceived each other in hopes of profit; what limit is there to those who destroy morality and ruin education? How much more serious is the problem when the path of adventurous profiteering is publicly espoused and pursued; under these conditions, how could we hope for the world's morals and customs to be upright, and not be thin and weak?"

When Colonel John Boyd, a remarkable unsung hero in American military history who revolutionized American military practice and policy by writing the first manual on jet aerial combat, spearheading the design of the F-15 and F-16, teaching the U.S. Marine Corps how to fight on the ground and shaping the tactics which won the Gulf War, was hiring someone to work for him in the Air Force he would tell him the following (*Boyd: The Fighter Pilot Who Changed the Art of War*, by Robert Coram): "You are at a point in your life where you have to make a choice about what kind of person you are going to be. There are two career paths in front of you, and you have to choose which path you will follow. One path leads to promotions, titles, and positions of distinctions. To achieve success down that path, you have to conduct yourself a certain way. You must go along with the system and show that you are a better team player than your competitors. The other path leads to doing things that are truly significant for the Air Force, but the rewards will quite often be a kick in the stomach because you have to cross swords with the party line on occasion. You can't go down both paths, you have to choose. So, do you want to be a man of distinction or do you want to do things that really influence the shape of the Air Force? To be or to do, that is the question."

This is the type of decision you often have in front of you with your life, namely to do what is right or something wrong and be rewarded with money or a promotion.

You also always have a choice of making a living, or living purposefully by performing a personal mission of some significance or labor of love with social benefits. The choice is up to you whether or not to reorient your life toward the virtues and causes you believe in. Why not toss the dice high, and risk embarking upon a road of significance even though you know it will entail difficulties? No outcome is fated in life because *you can create your own fate*, so it depends upon your efforts.

Use Your New Tools

You now have in your power the tools to more effectively pursue any goals and objectives you may want in life, including higher profits if that is what you want. You have the tools and technology to get things done much quicker and faster, and you now actually have a higher chance of achieving what you desire. With your new powers of productivity, may the goals you choose to seek in life truly be worthy of your vitality, time, money and ethics.

REFERENCES

The 168 Hour Week: Living Life Your Way, by Kevin Hogan
The 4-Hour Workweek: Escape 9-5, Live Anywhere, and Join the New Rich, by Timothy Ferriss.
Automatic Wealth for Grads, by Michael Masterson.
The Effective Executive, by Peter Drucker.
The E-Myth, by Michael Gerber.
Family Fortunes: How to Build Family Wealth and Hold on to It for 100 Years, by Bill Bonner and Will Bonner.
Four Lessons, by Liao Fan.
Getting Things Done, by David Allen.
How I Raised Myself from Failure to Success in Selling, by Frank Bettger.
How to Win Friends and Influence People, by Dale Carnegie.
How to Write a Million Dollar Unique Selling Proposition, by Bill Bodri.
Make it Big! 49 Rules for Building a Life of Extreme Success, by Frank McKinney.
Mastering the Rockefeller Habits, by Verne Harnish.
Mencius, Volume One, translated by D. C. Lau.
Move Forward: Powerful Strategies for Creating Better Outcomes in Life, by Bill Bodri.
The Pledge: Your Master Plan for an Abundant Life, by Michael Masterson.
The Story of Chinese Zen, by Nan Huai-Chin.
Super Investing: 5 Proven Methods for Beating the Market and Retiring Rich, by Bill Bodri.

The Talent Code: Greatness Isn't Born. It's Grown. Here's How, by Daniel Coyle.

Think and Grow Rich, by Napoleon Hill.

Thinking, Fast and Slow, by Daniel Kahneman.

The Ultimate Sales Machine, by Chet Homes.

Visualization Power, by Bill Bodri.

What They Don't Teach You at Harvard Law School, by Mark McCormick.

The Wisdom of Andrew Carnegie as Told to Napoleon Hill, by Napoleon Hill.

ABOUT THE AUTHOR

Bill Bodri is the author of several books on business performance, investing, health and self-help including:

- *Move Forward: Powerful Strategies for Creating Better Outcomes in Life*
- *How to Create a Million Dollar Unique Selling Proposition*
- *Breakthrough Strategies of Wall Street Traders: 17 Remarkable Traders Reveal Their Top Performing Investment Strategies*
- *Super Investing: 5 Proven Methods for Beating the Market and Retiring Rich*
- *High Yield Investments, Hard Assets and Asset Protection Strategies*
- *Super Cancer Fighters*
- *The Little Book of Meditation*
- *Look Younger, Live Longer*
- *Visualization Power*

The author can be contacted for speeches or interviews through wbodri@gmail.com.

Made in the USA
Coppell, TX
03 April 2023

15157865R00052